D1439073

BRIGHTON

Eric Underwood

BRIGHTON

'The world is eternally fresh; and,
if we moderns pine and fret and grudge
at it for having lost its ancient
earthly Paradise, then, in that delusion,
we condemn ourselves to the saddest
Paradise Lost that ever was.'

G. G. Coulton, *The Mediaeval Village*

B. T. Batsford Ltd,
London

First published 1978
Copyright © Eric Underwood 1978
Printed by J. W. Arrowsmith Ltd, Bristol
for the publishers B. T. Batsford Ltd
4 Fitzhardinge St, London W1H 0AH
ISBN 0 7134 0895 2

Contents

Acknowledgements

Among the many to whom the author owes thanks are Mr Leslie J. Whitehead for a personal description of the Springfield Road excavation (Chapter II); Mr and Mrs J. W. Ash for a conducted tour of Patcham Place and Mr David Campion for details of his family's history (Chapter IV); Sue and John Farrant for expert guidance on Chapter V; M. Claude Benoit for introducing him to La Garde's *Brighton* (Chapter VII); Mr John Carden for access to family records (Chapter X); Mr Anthony Dale for a briefing on the formation of the Regency Society of Brighton and Hove (Chapter XI); Miss Caroline Dudley and Dr Patrick Conner of Brighton Museum and Art Gallery; Miss S. P. Dalley of the University of Sussex Library and the staffs of the London Library, the East Sussex Record Office and the Brighton and Hove Reference Libraries. Most especially is he grateful to his wife, Kathleen, for those insights which can come only from one who is 'native here, and to the manner born'.

All the illustrations with the exception of those mentioned below are published by permission of The Royal Pavilion, Art Gallery and Museums, Brighton. For Nos 22 and 23 the author is indebted to the kindness of Mrs Millard, of 9 Cownwy Court, Rottingdean, granddaughter of Mr Frederick Thomas and daughter of Mr George Thomas, both of whom appear in these photographs. Nos 20, 21, 24, 25 and 26 are from the justifiably famous collection of Mr J. S. Gray. No. 2 was taken by the author and Nos 6, 11, 12 and 13 are from the publisher's reference library.

The jacket design is a section of 'Holiday Time at the Seaside—The Midday Promenade in front of the King's Road, Brighton' (*c.* 1895) by G. Durand. This is among the fine collection of Brighton prints in 'The Cricketers' hotel, Black Lion Street, and is reproduced by permission of Miss Winnie Sexton.

List of Illustrations

CHAPTER ONE

'Curious for Antiquities'

'The art of Biography
Is different from Geography.
Geography is about maps,
But Biography is about chaps.'
E. C. Bentley: *Biography for Beginners*

All towns, like most people, become more interesting as you learn something of their past. No town which has the sea beside it can ever be boring; nor can a town that is built on hills. Brighton has both hills and sea to offer refreshment to the eye and, moreover, wears one period of her history where even the most casual observer can see it—in her Regency squares and crescents and in the theatrical bizarrerie of the Royal Pavilion.

But the human adventure in Brighton did not begin or end with George III's wayward son. A flint implement found in the cliffs east of the town shows there were men living in the locality a quarter of a million years ago—long before the scouring out of the English Channel gave rise to that insularity which has provided a fascinating spectrum of advantages and problems ever since.

Since history is largely a record of man's accommodation to geography it is best to begin by describing where Brighton stands on the map.

It is in Sussex, the main features of which—reading from north to south—are: the Forest Ridge, running west to east; an inland plain—the Weald; a second range of hills, roughly parallel to the first—the South Downs; and a narrow coastal strip.

The South Downs form the chalk ridge which runs through Sussex like a backbone from the Hampshire border to Beachy Head. Their northern slopes are abrupt; their southern slopes are gradual. The coastal plain, 12 miles wide at its western end, narrows progressively as one moves eastward until Downs and sea finally converge and the white cliffs begin. It was in this furthest eastern tip of the plain, in a spot conveniently sheltered from the north and east winds, that the settlement we now know as

9

Brighton was originally built. One valley or 'combe' comes south-
westerly out of the Downs and another in a south-easterly direction to
meet and lead down to an area of level ground, known as the Steine, which
lay immediately east of the mediaeval town but is the focal point of modern Brighton.

An inconsiderable and probably intermittent stream, the Wellsbourne,
used to flow down the Steine to the sea, but the nearest rivers are the Adur
six miles to the west and the Ouse eight miles to the east.

It is the sea that has shaped Brighton's history down the centuries. It
has provided a livelihood to fishermen, merchant mariners and—on
occasion—smugglers and pirates. Time and time again it has destroyed
large areas of the town by gradual erosion or sudden storm. It has brought
in immigrants, raiders, invaders and refugees and, when Imperial Rome
abandoned Britain, carried thousands of British emigrants to Brittany
and Normandy. William the Conquerer's troops built a strongpoint on
the chalk ridge behind the town and armies crossed in the opposite direction when Henry II, more a European ruler than an English king, held
sway over the western half of France from the English Channel to the
Pyrenees. During the Hundred Years' War and the Tudor wars with both
France and Spain, its people were kept on constant alert, ready to fire the
signal beacons and ring an alarm from the belfry of the parish church; a
pattern to be repeated—with modern variations—in the two European
wars of this century.

There will always be some who will agree with Sir Philip Sidney, the
Elizabethan soldier-poet, when he said (in his *Apologie for Poetrie* and with
his tongue very much in his cheek) that the historian is 'loaden with old
mouse-eaten records, authorising himself for the most part upon other
histories, whose greatest authorities are built uppon the notable foundation of heresay, having much ado to accord differing writers, and to
prick truth out of partiality; better acquainted with a thousand years ago
than with the present age, and yet better knowing how this world goeth,
than how his owne wit runneth; curious for antiquities and inquisitive of
novelties; a wonder to young folkes, and a tyrant in table talk.'

But I think there are more—particularly as this bewildering century
enters its final quarter—who find the reading of history an invaluable,
perhaps indispensable, aid to sanity; who recognise that some acquaintance with the thoughts and deeds of men and women long (or even
recently) dead is the ideal antidote to the latest news-bulletin and the
ominous in-tray. There is no better way of putting the apparently un-

bearable into perspective than to recognise (with George Macaulay Trevelyan) 'the quasi-miraculous fact that once, on this earth . . . walked other men and women, as actual as we are today, thinking their own thoughts, swayed by their passions, but now all gone, one generation vanishing into another, gone as utterly as we ourselves shall shortly be gone, like ghosts at cockcrow'.*

I have written this book with several types of reader in mind. All residents of long standing are enthusiasts for Brighton and many of them are enthusiasts for its history. For them there is newly available information—for instance on Brighton in the early 1700's—that has not appeared in earlier works and also an illuminating commentary on the social scene in the 1820's by a French author—the Comte de La Garde—who has been undeservedly neglected by most Brighton historians.

But I have also borne in mind the needs of the newly-arrived resident of Brighton and of the temporary visitor (especially if he or she is one of those coming in increasing numbers from mainland Europe and North America). I hope the book will do three things for them: enable them to look at the town as a whole with a more interested eye; introduce them to some of the literature on the subject, which is rich and varied; and indicate buildings and places that will give added depth to what they read.

Where buildings and places are concerned I have not confined my recommendations to the town limits. It goes without saying that I have drawn examples from the contiguous town of Hove, whose frontier with Brighton has been obscured by bricks and mortar for so many decades that only the most delicate of social antennae can detect it. It should also be explained that many of the place-names used are those of former villages that now lie within the boundaries of the two towns; some are still recognisably separate, some not. Brighton has claimed Preston, Withdean, Hollingbury, Patcham, Stanmer, Coldean, Moulsecoomb, Bevendean, Falmer, Woodingdean, Ovingdean, Rottingdean and Saltdean; Hove has Blatchington, Hangleton and Portslade. (Sussex place-names ending in -coomb or -combe, -dean and -ford are like the 'Shibboleth' of the Old Testament: the way you pronounce them shows whether you are local-born or not. Locals put the emphasis on the final syllable; immigrants on the first . . . until and unless corrected. Stanmer is another pitfall, being spoken as if it were spelt S-t-a-m-m-e-r). Where a building or site

---

*An Autobiography and Other Essays (Longmans, Green & Co., 1949)

relevant to the particular period exists in neither town I have suggested, whenever possible, an alternative in that area of the Downs or southern Weald which can be reached in a day's visit, whether by public transport or private car.

There is yet a third class of reader I should like to reach; for rather different reasons. It consists of those who have never visited Brighton and will perhaps never have the opportunity of doing so, and yet enjoy the past in the way Trevelyan did. To them I would say that—although the nature of events will differ—histories just as curious as Brighton's can be written about any town on earth if one digs deep enough in the right places. If this is new territory for them they will be gratified to find what a friendly race librarians and archivists are and how briskly our ancestors step out from old wills and yellowing newspaper-files.

In writing such a book as this one is inevitably struck by the fact that each succeeding century provides more material than the one before it for the historian to work on. Before the invention of writing only bones, pottery, weapons, tools and cave-paintings were left for him to ponder; later the remains of buildings; then manuscripts—chronicles, diaries, letters; then the infinite variety of printed matter. Until comparatively recent times there were severe limitations on the quantity and type of material produced. Much of the population was illiterate and so unable to speak to posterity with its own voice. Again only the well-to-do could have their portraits painted; a peasant would have no idea of what his great-grandparents looked like.

The first significant change came with the invention of the still-camera. It not only gave a much more factual impression of events and people, reducing to a marked degree that element of interpretation (or distortion) which must inevitably enter into a drawing or painting (have you noticed how the camera revealed the *crumpled* look of the clothes worn by Victorian sitters?); it also provided portraiture, throughout all classes of society, on a scale that had hitherto been inconceivable.

Now, unless there is a cataclysm or family bonfires become a regular custom, everyone will not only be able to see what his ancestors looked like in repose, but to study their mannerisms and gait on moving film and to hear their voices on tape. This may or may not be welcome to the family concerned (some 'great' actors over whom the elderly enthuse can be pathetic on archive film); it will certainly inundate the historian of the future with material. Should we envy or commiserate?

CHAPTER TWO

Before the Norman Conquest

'And see you the marks that show and fade,
  Like shadows on the Downs?
O they are the lines the Flint Men made,
  To guard their wondrous towns.'

Rudyard Kipling, *Puck of Pook's Hill*

Two miles east of the centre of Brighton, at a point in the cliffs known as Black Rock, is the town's latest engineering project. A semi-circle of immense concrete caissons has been sunk on to the seabed to create what will become the largest yacht harbour in Europe.

Turn your back to the sea and climb inland for a mile to the grandstands of Brighton's racecourse, at the top of Whitehawk Hill, and you will be standing on Brighton's oldest piece of engineering.

Its outlines are now much obscured by the levellings and adaptations consequent upon the site being used for horse-racing since Regency times, but it is what is called 'a causewayed camp' of the New Stone Age and was built about 5,000 years ago. It consisted of four concentric rings of earth ramparts and ditches, the outermost being 900 feet in diameter, so that the whole area comprises nearly 12 acres. There are only a dozen such 'camps' in Britain (four of them in Sussex), although eight others are known in Germany and Belgium.

The adjective 'causewayed' is used because the ditches were not continuous, being crossed at intervals by bridges of uncut chalk.

Although Whitehawk is often referred to as a 'camp', it is not now generally thought of as a defensive earthwork, but—in the words of Barry Cunliffe, Professor of European Archaeology at Oxford University—as a place 'where meetings could be held, gifts exchanged and rituals practised'. It was one of 'the communal centres of tribal society'.* The earthworks may well have served as corrals on these occasions, for although the

---

*Barry Cunliffe: *The Regni* (Duckworth, 1973)

animal bones found here do not include those of the horse there are many of small longhorn oxen and of pigs; some of sheep and goats.

What kind of people gathered here—longer before the birth of Christ than we are after it? A vividly suggestive picture is conjured up by E. Cecil Curwen who excavated the site in 1928. 'Life at Whitehawk Camp must have been at a very low level', he writes.* 'We have spoken of the Neolithic folk as enjoying the elements of material civilisation, but this does not imply that they were in the least degree civilised in their manners. In fact the excavations here suggest that the reverse was the case . . . the third ditch disclosed some sordid secrets . . . among the animal bones we found parts of the brain pans of human skulls, three small fragments of which had been charred in the fire; while scattered about the rest of this part of the ditch—all in the same dark layer—we came across three more human brain pans and one or two other bits of human bone. All the five individuals here represented were young; the oldest was not much, if at all over 20, the youngest was about six. What were these children's skulls doing round this domestic hearth unless the occupant of this piece of ditch was a cannibal?'

One's first reaction (as Curwen's was) is one of revulsion, and then of incredulity. Yet survival then and for many centuries afterwards was as chancy a business in Northern Europe as it can still be in Africa and Asia. It may have been desperate hunger rather than perverse appetite that drove the Whitehawk men to eat human flesh—as European peasants were to do during the famines of the Dark and Middle Ages; some historians suggest, quite plausibly, that stories like that of Hänsel and Gretel embalm folk-memories of such horrors. Even in our own day newspapers have described how the survivors of an air-crash in the Andes stayed alive by eating their dead fellow-passengers.

On a clear day—and preferably not a race day—Whitehawk Camp is an admirable spot for a preliminary reconnaissance of the early history of this part of Sussex. Urban Brighton may seem to hem you in as you look down the steep eastern slope to a Council housing estate and westward to the Victorian workhouse, but only two miles away in a north-north-westerly direction can be seen the Iron Age fort of Hollingbury, islanded in a municipal golf-course. Six miles off, to the north-west of Whitehawk is another Iron Age fort, one of the most famous in Britain; spectacularly sited on the 711-foot-high Devil's Dyke, it commands a

*E. Cecil Curwen: *The Archaeology of Sussex* (Methuen, 1954)

superb view of the Weald. West-north-west and 12 miles away, you can see Cissbury Ring where—when the causewayed camp was built—flints were mined with picks made from antlers and shovels that had been the shoulder-blades of oxen.

Finally, just over 12 miles away, in a north-westerly direction from where you are standing, you will see one of the best-known landmarks in Sussex: Chanctonbury Ring. Easily identifiable on an otherwise bare sky-line by its thick, well-rounded clump of beeches, it stands 750 feet above sa-level. There was a Celtic temple on this hill-top and later a Roman one; the supernatural associations of a particular spot tended to persist, even though new gods elbowed out the old.

Since the invention of the wheel, men have preferred to travel in valleys rather than on hills, so that it is still possible—along the South Downs Way—to follow on foot the chalky ridge-tracks that linked these places together. Anyone doing so cannot help noticing the frequent occurrence of grass-grown mounds, the burial-barrows or 'tumuli' of the ancient peoples. The long barrows are those of the Stone Age men; the round ones date from the Bronze Age.

An early Bronze Age barrow stood until 1856 in what was then known as Coney Burrow Field but is now the back-garden of No. 13, Palmeira Avenue, Hove. Fortunately for posterity a local antiquarian, Barclay Phillips, Esq., was on the *qui vive* when the time came for progress to march over it.

'Rising from a perfectly level plain', he writes, 'and being unconnected with any other hills, it always presented the appearance of an artificial mound, and therefore, when, some years ago, a road was cut through it to the Hove Station of the Brighton and Portsmouth Railway, I was anxious to learn whether any antiquities had been met with; but not any were then found. Now, however, all doubt on the subject has been set at rest, and the hillock proved to be a Barrow, or monumental mound erected over the remains of an ancient British chieftain. Labourers have recently been employed in removing the earth of this hill, and last week, on reaching the centre of the mound, about two yards west of the road leading to Hove Station, and about nine feet below the surface, dug out a rude coffin between six and seven feet long. On exposure to the atmosphere the boards immediately crumbled away; but a few of the knots remained and proved to be of oak'.*

---

* Quoted in *History of Brighthelmston* by J. E. Erredge (1862)

The coffin contained 'small fragments of bone' and some 'curious relics'—intended for the chieftain's use in the other world—which are now housed with Brighton Museum.

Notable among them is a small double-headed axe of charcoal-grey volcanic stone, one of the finest examples of its kind. It was more probably a symbol of office—as a sceptre would be— than a working tool or weapon and one only has to run one's fingers over its satisfying curves and impeccable smoothness for the skill and pride of the man who made it to live again. The other objects are a small whetstone with a hole bored through it; a bronze spear-head which, says Mr Phillips, was 'very much oxidised and so brittle that it broke into halves as it was being taken out of the ground'; and a cup carved from a block of red Baltic amber.

About 1500 B.C. there was a new influx of immigrants from the Continent who initiated a more settled form of agriculture than their predecessors'. It was based on the plough and soon there was a scatter of farms all over the Downs and the coastal plain. They used a wider range of bronze implements and worked the metal in more sophisticated ways. One ornament of distinctive shape is known as 'a Brighton loop' because 17 of the 24 recorded specimens were found within six miles of the town and all but two within a radius of 16 miles, making it probable that they were all made by the same craftsman or group of craftsmen. E. Cecil Curwen, while admitting they resemble 'a peculiar kind of bracelet', thought them 'too small to fit over any but the most slender wrists' and 'very heavy and uncomfortable to wear' (Miss Caroline Dudley, Brighton Museum's Keeper of Archaeology, was good enough to try one on for me and seemed to suffer no discomfort in so doing).

About 500 B.C. another wave of immigrants from north-western Europe began which was to continue until it culminated in the Roman occupation. They brought a new metal with them—iron—which displaced bronze quite abruptly; there was none of the gradual transition which marked the flint-bronze phase. The superior virtues of iron were recognised immediately.

It was during this period that the great hill-forts of Sussex came into existence, structures of increasing ingenuity being built in succeeding centuries on the same sites. At Hollingbury, for example, a comparatively simple earthwork of the Early Iron Age preceded the fort of 250 B.C. whose outline we see today.

Curwen,* writing of this type of military architecture (which Julius

---
*Op. cit.

Caesar was to encounter in Gaul two centuries later), says: 'Their present ruinous condition gives very little idea as to their former strength, for however high their grassy ramparts are today they can easily be scaled by an active man. In their original form, however, the walls were built of chalk rubble contained in a timber framework in such a way as to present a vertical face to the enemy, and a little distance in front of this there was a wide and deep trench which would present an almost insuperable obstacle to an assailant without scaling ladders'.*

During the first century B.C. there were yet more newcomers from the mainland of Europe, impelled by the westward push of the Teuton tribes and later by Roman armies advancing steadily northwards to extend their hold over Gaul. Finally Julius Caesar led expeditions into Britain in 55 and 54 B.C., but only Kent, Essex and Hertfordshire were seriously affected and, after what modern generals would call a 'demonstration', he withdrew.

But the *pax Romana* could never become a reality in Gaul while there was an independent offshore island where a people linked by blood and sympathy with the mainland tribes was only too ready to give refuge and support to dissident elements within the Empire.

In A.D. 43 Rome struck. A month's campaign gave her complete control of south-eastern England. Various evidences revealed by archaeologists suggest that the area of Sussex which now includes Brighton escaped untouched by these hostilities. There are clear signs of old hill-forts being refurbished for effective defence east of Lewes and west of Chichester, but no such preparations seem to have been made in the area between these two points.

This provides a strong probability that the territory was ruled by someone who—like the cannier rajahs in the days of John Company or like Quisling in Norway—had a shrewd idea which side would win and decided to join it. Written sources tell us that, at about this time, there appeared on the British scene a local bigwig who called himself Tiberius Claudius Cogidubnus. The Roman historian Tacitus mentions him briefly and a Latin inscription found in Chichester refers to him as an 'imperial legate'. The magnificent Roman palace excavated in recent years at Fishbourne near Chichester was almost certainly built for this British 'client king' somewhere between A.D. 75 and 80.

For two centuries Britain experienced the Roman way of ordering society and was almost completely insulated from barbarian interference by Hadrian's Wall and the strongpoints along the Rhine. Roman Sussex was prosperous farming country, with only one town, Chichester, from which the great road we know as Stane Street ran over the Downs to London. It can still be clearly seen on the top of Bignor Hill, near Arundel, and from there one can look down at the famous Roman villa in Bignor village. One of the largest in Britain, it was probably the residence of a 'Romanised' British landowner; it can still show us its elaborately patterned mosaic floors (including one depicting a gladiatorial combat by Cupids!), its painted walls and central heating.

Because of extensive urbanisation in the nineteenth and twentieth centuries it is more difficult to assess the extent of Roman involvement with the Brighton area than it would be in more open country, but there are known to have been a large country house at Southwick, a farm at West Blatchington and a building of some kind at Preston. One matter on which there has been some doubt is whether or not there was an east-west road south of the Downs—passing through the site of present-day Brighton—as there was on the northern side.

The road system of the county was extensive (and of a quality that would not be seen again until the end of the eighteenth century) because Sussex was a valuable larder, supplying corn and mutton not only to London, but to the garrisons on Hadrian's Wall and even oversea to Gaul. It was for this reason that a secondary road was built from the capital to the Brighton area by way of Lewes.

An interesting new light was thrown on these matters by the discovery of certain Romano-British remains which until recently were to be seen, not in Brighton Museum, but—with the unpredictability which is part of this town—in an office over a garage.*

When, in 1876, new houses were being built at Preston, pits containing human skeletons were found in what was to be known as Springfield Road. In the following year remains of a Romano-British building— described as a 'villa' at the time—were uncovered, together with an urn containing human bones. In 1880 yet another urn burial was found in the same area.

There the matter stood until, in 1962, as part of a reconstruction programme for their garage, the Endeavour Motor Co. Ltd, began to demolish Nos 1, 3 and 5, Springfield Road. One of their directors, Mr Leslie J. Whitehead, was an amateur archaeologist and very much alive to the possibility that there could be further finds. When a mechanical digger

---

*They were not incorporated into the Museum's collection until 1977.

brought up a funerary urn, some pottery and fragments of a glass bottle from the trench it was digging, he determined to spend the whole of one Sunday exploring the trench (which was to be concreted the next day).

Mr Whitehead, a friend (Mr Potter) and two 13-year-old schoolboys (John Taylor and John Potter) assembled a number of objects interesting enough to justify eight hours' digging and sieving under a hot sun: the remains of a bronze-bound wooden box which appeared to have contained bones; a variety of pots; a square glass bottle; a top-hat-shaped glass container of the kind Roman ladies used for eye make-up; and, to quote Mr Whitehead, human bones 'turning up in ever-increasing quantities'.

But the most exciting finds were a hanging wall-lamp of iron and two figurines of reddish pipe-clay, all in an excellent state of preservation. The figurines, of a type rare on this side of the Channel, were busts, 4½ inches high, of young, handsome women. Whether they represented the dead ladies themselves or goddesses who would help them on their journey to the nether world is not known. What is certain is that they were importations from the Allier district, near Vichy.

This new evidence, combined with that gathered over 80 years before, strengthened Mr Whitehead's belief that the building on this site had not been a villa but a temple associated with a cemetery. The existence of a Roman cemetery at Hassocks, six miles away, on the east-west road north of the Downs, had been known for a number of years and there is a striking similarity between the urns and other pottery found at the two sites. Because it was the Roman custom to site cemeteries beside busy roads this helps to substantiate the theory of a lateral road on the seaward side of the Downs.

The long spell of security and prosperity began to break down in the last quarter of the third century. Barbarian tribes were making land attacks on Gaul and seaborne raids on both sides of the Channel. For 100 years and more periods of barbarian harassment and civil disorder alternated with spells of relative quiet, but the latter became less and less frequent as increasing internal dissension and mounting external pressures weakened the Empire. Legion after legion was withdrawn from Britain to deal with crises in the more central provinces until in A.D. 407—for the first time in 350 years—not a single Roman soldier was left on British soil. When, three years later, the Britons appealed to the Emperor Honorius for help against invading Saxons his letter of reply told them they would have to 'look after their own defences' which, apparently, they managed to do for a time, since the historian Zosimus records that 'the Britons took up arms and, braving danger for their own independence, freed their cities from the barbarians threatening them'.

But in 430, following a practice they had learned from their Roman masters, they began employing these same Saxons as mercenaries against attacks from Picts and Scots.

They were soon to discover, as Rome had done, that while this is a perfectly satisfactory technique when your frontiers are pushing outward and your star is in the ascendant, it is fatal in a time of decline. In 442 the Saxons rebelled against their employers and began to overrun the country, and in 457 (or possibly 447)* reinforcements landed, under a leader called Aella who was to conquer all the country between Chichester and Pevensey, so that it became known by the name is still bears today, the land of the South Saxons—Sussex.

The Anglo-Saxon Chronicle tells us that 'Aella and his three sons, Cymen, Wlencing and Cissa, came to Britain in three ships and landed at a place known as Cymens-ora, and there slew many Britons, driving some in flight to the wood called Andreds-lea' (presumably the thickly forested area north of the Downs). The Chronicle also records that eight years later he fought the Britons 'on the bank of the Mearcradsburn' [i.e. 'river-of-the-frontier'] and six years after that 'besieged Andreds-cester [Pevensey] and slew all the Britons who lived there'.

No one can be certain which was the 'river-of-the-frontier'; the Adur and the Ouse have both been suggested but some commentators opt for the Arun which would extend Aella's kingdom a further 11 miles to the west. Whichever theory is correct the disposition of pagan Saxon burials of this period indicates that Aella's people were thick on the ground in the coastal strip of East Sussex and that what is now Brighton formed part of the area.

A book by historian John Morris** has added a new and seductive ingredient to the life of Aella and therefore, by association, to the history of Brighton. After their initial setbacks the Britons rallied and fought with the ferocity of despair for 35 years until they finally inflicted so decisive a defeat on the Saxons that the invaders' advance was halted and their frontiers could extend no further west or north for another 100 years. This final battle was at Badon, near Bath, and the Saxon forces were led by

---

*The accepted date used to be that given in the Anglo-Saxon Chronicle—A.D. 477; but recent researches have set it 20 or even 30 years earlier.
**The Age of Arthur (Weidenfeld and Nicolson, 1973)

Aella—by no means the most powerful of the Saxon kinglets but apparently chosen because he was the most senior in years.

The interesting question is: Who was the general of the opposing army, the British paladin who stemmed the pagan tide? John Morris contends that it was Artorius, a Romanised British squire from just such a country estate as Bignor, whose masterly use of cavalry tactics (the Saxons fought always on foot) had raised him to the chief command.

Artorius is, of course, none other than King Arthur whose adventures, says John Morris, constitute 'one of the great tales in Europe, told again and again in all lands that speak a Latin or Germanic language', to celebrate 'a strong and just ruler who protected his people against barbarism without and oppression within'. He has written an erudite, enthralling and persuasive book to support his theory, but as an honest professional does not conceal the fact that Gildas, a chronicler who lived in Arthur's presumed lifetime does not mention his name, which appears first 'about 80 years after his time' in a Welsh poet's tribute to a dead warrior. Whether Arthur is fact or myth he so exactly embodies the combination of idealism and pugnacity which Europe has always admired that, as this author says, each generation has 'clothed Arthur in the ideas of its own day'.

Sussex was the last of the Anglo-Saxon kingdoms to forsake the old pagan gods and embrace Christianity. Its conversion by St Wilfred did not take place until the end of the 7th century, almost 100 years after St Augustine had converted the neighbouring kingdom of Kent. Some authorities consider that Brighton owed its name in its original form to one of St Wilfred's priests. For much of its history it was known as Brighthelmstone, thought to be a corruption of 'Beorthelm's-tun', the farm of Beorthelm.

Sussex continued under Saxon rule for 600 years. Their secular buildings were of wood and have left little trace, but to honour their new god they built in stone. A lovely little Saxon church can be seen in the village of Clayton (close beside the northern entrance of the railway tunnel that takes the Brighton line through the Downs) and another fine example of their work is the tower of the Church of St Mary at Sompting, just outside Worthing.

But Brighton and Hove provide two fascinating examples of the way the pagan past can persist in the behaviour of ordinary people—without any prompting by the scholarly—for astonishingly long periods of time.

It is easy to forget that the Bronze Age barrow levelled by the Victorian 'improvers' of Hove was over 2,000 years old when the Saxons came. As we noticed of Chanctonbury Ring, the 'ghostly' associations of a particular spot tended to outlive political change and E. C. Curwen mentions that right up to the time of its destruction in 1856 the barrow was 'visited every Good Friday by hundreds of young people who used to play Kiss-in-the-Ring and other games—a custom which no doubt had its origin in very ancient ceremonial observances'.

Considering the time of year at which the game was played it almost certainly had its origins in a fertility rite designed to ingratiate the participants with Eostre, the goddess of Spring. When Pope Gregory the Great sent missionaries to England, he showed a very shrewd appreciation of just how far human nature can be stretched in its absorption of new ideas and was prepared to allow the islanders to retain a little pagan sugar if they would swallow the Christian pill.

He said, for example, 'Do not . . . pull down the temples. Destroy the idols; purify the buildings with holy water, set relics there; and let them become temples of the true God. Thus the people will have no need to change their places of concourse; and where of old they would want to sacrifice cattle to demons, thither let them continue to resort on the day of the saint to whom the church is dedicated, and slay their beasts no longer as a sacrifice, but for a social meal in honour of Him whom they now worship.'

And, in the same way that—on Gregory's advice—pagan feasts were bowdlerised into 'Church Ales', so many former religious ceremonies became ostensibly innocent sports; and the old goddess Eostre gave her name to Easter.

Although Hove's Kiss-in-the-Ring is mentioned briefly by one contemporary local historian,* no detailed description of it survives. Fortunately the game was played elsewhere in similar circumstances and observed by other Victorian authors.

Cockneys played it on Easter Monday at Blackheath (again not far from a tumulus), a fact recorded by a journeyman engineer, Thomas Wright, whose book *The Great Unwashed* was published in 1868.

'As Easter is avowedly an outdoor holiday', he writes, 'a holiday to be spent, if possible, in some green spot of the earth . . . those of the unwashed whose lot it is to dwell in stony, smoky, overcrowded towns and cities are naturally among its most enthusiastic devotees . . . . To them there are fewer places that offer greater attractions than Greenwich . . . .

---

* J. A. Erredge, Op. cit.

Early on Easter Monday morning Greenwich begins to show tokens of the coming invasion of pleasure-seeking. The park and Blackheath (which, as Londoners are aware, adjoins the park) are the chief centres of attraction . . . . On entering the park it becomes evident that

"On with the dance, let the joy be unconfined"

is the animating principle of action among the assembled thousands of smiling, happy-looking holiday-makers . . . . After dancing, kiss-in-the-ring is the game most in vogue with those in the park, and especially with courting couples, who in it find a means of combined love and amusement.'

An even more evocative description is given by that eccentric Victorian civil servant and minor poet, Arthur J. Munby,* who studied English working girls (one of whom he married secretly) as an ethnologist would a primitive African tribe.

The game he describes had apparently broken with its Easter connection and was played on any fine summer evening, but otherwise it obviously followed much the same lines as Thomas Wright's.

In his diary for Wednesday, 10 July 1861, Munby writes: 'I went down to the Crystal Palace at five . . . then up to the slopes under the little wood, where a large circle had been formed for Kiss in the Ring.

'The women were chiefly shop girls and servants . . . a nice-looking girl came up, & saying "Are you in the ring, Sir?" offered me her favour—a leaf. I acquiesced; I caught and led her and kissed her: and stimulated by the feat, we joined the game; a young woman next to me linking her hand in mine with much simplicity, whereby I became part of the circle.

'I remained passive at first: but soon, one pretty girl after another, and several who were passées and plain (cooks, probably), came up, threw me the leaf in passing with an arch look and a smile, and dashed out of the ring and down the slope. These I had to pursue and reclaim; and good fleet runners many of them were . . . It is interesting to see how far things that would in a higher class be counted "liberties" are tolerated here, and even expected, without suspicion of evil. When, after a chase, you bear down full sail on your partner, you may seize her anyhow so as to detain her—for she is apt to break away—; and the collision often brings you to the ground together. Again, when this romping has ended in her sub-

---

*Derek Hudson: *Munby: Man of Two Worlds—The Life and Diaries of Arthur J. Munby 1828–1910* (John Murray, 1972)

mission, you place your arm around her waist, & lead her tenderly back to the ring, and when you get there, your kisses may be numerous, your embrace somewhat fervent . . . .'

In the Middle Ages and later the Church often showed signs of regretting Pope Gregory's liberal attitude and Rome would fulminate against these pastimes as bitterly as any Puritan. Zeger Van Espen, who became professor of Church law at the University of Louvain in 1675, wrote: 'If we consider those dances, leapings and skippings which are performed nowadays, especially in the country among persons of both sexes, it will be evident that they will exactly fit that which their Fathers have said about the dances and spectacles of their own day, and that, as St Charles Borromeo said, "such meetings are scarcely ever brought about without many and and most grievous offences against God" ' (among which he listed 'foul thoughts . . . fornication and adultery').

Thomas Wright mentions skipping as another form of Easter jollification and this survived in Brighton as a Good Friday custom among the fishermen and their families into the present century. It was called 'Long Rope Day' or 'Long Line Day' and in Victorian times the skipping-rope was dignified as 'an emblem of the rope Judas hanged himself with', which could be a rationalisation dating back to St Wilfred.

'In Brighton on this day', wrote F. E. Sawyer in *Sussex Archaeological Collections* (1883), 'the children in the back streets bring up ropes from the beach. One stands on the pavement on one side and one on the other while one skips in the middle of the street. Sometimes a pair (a boy and a girl) skip together and sometimes a great fat bathing-woman will take her place and skip as merrily as the grandsire does in Goldsmith's *"Traveller"*.' On Good Friday of that year 'burly navvies' were to be seen 'skipping actively' and on the Level (a local open space) 'there were scores of skippers'.

The tradition was maintained at the fish-market on the 'hard' near the Palace Pier until the mid-1920's when—for no particular reason that the older members of the fishing community can now identify—it lapsed.

CHAPTER THREE

Mediaeval and Tudor Wars

'His Valour's proofe, His Manly Vertue's Prayse,
Cannot be Marshall'd in this narrow Roome,
His brave Exploit in great King Henry's Dayes,
Among the Worthy hath a Worthier Tombe;
What time ye French Sought to have Sack't Sea-Foord,
This Pelham did Repell-em back Aboord.'

Epitaph to Sir Nicholas Pelham
in St Michael's Church, Lewes

Brighton's last Saxon overlord was Harold, the last of the Saxon kings. His death at Hastings on 14 October 1066, put a foreign king on the throne and introduced a ruling class who spoke a foreign language. The cows and sheep that the Saxon peasants tended in the fields became *boeuf* and *mouton* when they appeared on their lords' tables.

The barons and knights of Normandy, Brittany and Flanders who fought under William the Conqueror's flag were practical business men as well as warriors; to use the words of G. M. Trevelyan, they formed 'a joint-stock enterprise for the sharing out of the English lands'.*

And, like successful business men of our own day, they prided themselves on their efficiency. Modern calculations put the force that landed at no more than 12,000. To quote Trevelyan again: 'That a country of a million and a half people should have been subdued, robbed and permanently held down by so small a band, gives the measure of the political and military backwardness of the English system as compared to the Norman.'

Again, like any good business man. William believed in insurance and—as can be seen in the Bayeux Tapestry—his first act on landing was to build a castle, in which he could await reinforcements should the tide of battle turn against him. It was not one of the stone castles he was soon to

---

*G. M. Trevelyan: *A Shortened History of England* (Pelican, 1960)

make a familiar feature of the English landscape, but a much simpler structure known as 'motte-and-bailey'—not unlike the wooden forts that house the United States cavalry when they are fighting Indians in films about the Far West.

The bailey was a levelled piece of ground, oblong in shape, protected by a ditch and a fence. At one end, within this perimeter, was an artifical mound—the motte—made from the earth that had been dug to create the moat that ran all round it. Crowning the motte were a stockade (probably of undressed tree-trunks) and a wooden look-out tower. (It is believed that William was modern enough in his ideas to have brought with him a tower in pre-fabricated sections for rapid erection in the beachhead). Inside the outer fence of the bailey would be huts for the garrison and stables for their horses.

Seven miles from Brighton, in the county town of Lewes, there are still the handsome ruins of a stone castle, dominating the town and guarding the gap in the Downs through which the Ouse runs through to the sea. But, more interestingly perhaps, the remains of a motte-and-bailey (trad-itionally called Castle Rings) can be seen six miles to the north-west of Brighton, at the top of Edburton Hill.

It is easy to miss, for it lies just off the South Downs Way, the old ridge track that conservationists have preserved for those who still like to travel on their feet or on a horse's back. About halfway between the Devil's Dyke and Beeding Hill (where the ground drops away to the valley of the Adur) a line of electricity pylons climbs Edburton Hill on its way from the Weald to the power station at Portslade. From the highest pylon the Downs Way veers south in a slight 'bulge', but a rather faint footpath goes straight ahead and this leads to the motte-and-bailey. It is not in so perfect a con-dition as some (for instance, the really copy-book example at Parracombe on the southern edge of Exmoor), but it is still worth a visit, standing as it does on the crown of what Nikolaus Pevsner calls 'one of the most sheer and spectacular bits of the whole Downs escarpment . . . The hill might as well be 5,000 feet high instead of 500.'*

If you stand on the earthworks it at once becomes clear why this site was chosen. The sharp drop of ground to the north gave the garrison an unin-terrupted view of the great forest of the Weald, which was the most likely hiding place for any Saxon resistance groups. East and west they could survey a great sweep of the Downs from Chanctonbury to Wolstenbury

---

Sussex (Penguin, 1965)

and their view to the south would give them early warning of any trouble brewing on the coast. Even today it can seem a lonely spot as the sun goes down and it must have been even more so to a Norman on sentry-go in the months after the Battle of Hastings when those of the Saxon militia who had escaped with their lives were back in their farms but still kept their weapons stowed away in the thatch.

However, there is written evidence which suggests that the peasantry in the Brighton area gave little trouble but accepted their change of overlord with the sullen resignation that Kipling describes in his story, 'Young Men at the Manor'.*

Twenty years after the Conquest, William, who—although unable to write even his own name—was a giant of administration, instituted the compilation of a document which was in intention a mammoth survey of national resources for tax purposes although it also served as a census which was to be unrivalled for another 800 years: the Domesday Book, so called because the thoroughness of the inquisition was thought to rival that which would occur on Judgement Day.

Tax-collectors have never been popular and when the Anglo-Saxon Chronicle refers to Domesday Book it strikes the same plaintive note that rings through leading articles and letters-to-the-editor on related subjects in our own day: ' . . . he required to be written down . . . what and how much in land or cattle had every man who was holding land in England, and how much it was worth. So very closely did he cause it to be investigated, that there was not a single hide, nor a yard of land, nor even—it is shameful to tell though it seemed no shame to him to do—an ox nor a cow nor a pig that was overlooked and not included in the record. And all the records were brought to him afterwards.'

In return for services the Conqueror had bestowed many estates on his son-in-law William de Warenne, Earl of Surrey. In addition to possessions in other countries he held from the king the 'Rape of Lewes', which constituted one-sixth of the whole area of Sussex. The Brighton area (or Bristelmstune, as the Norman clerks recorded it) was divided into three manors held by three knights, who were the tenants and vassals of William de Warenne. Domesday Book tells us not only that there was already in 1086 a church in the manor of Bristelmstune-Atlyngworth, it gives us the value of each manor in the time of Edward the Confessor ('tempore regis Edwardi' or T.R.E.); what it was worth 'afterwards', i.e.

Puck of Pook's Hill

after the Conquest; and what its value had become by the time of the 1086 survey.

Bristelmstune-Michelham, for example: 'In the time of King Edward it was worth £10, and afterwards £8: now £12' (or, in the Latin shorthand of this eminently business-like document: 'T.R.E. val't x lib. et post 8 lib: modo 12 lib.').

All three manors together were worth £28. 12s. in Edward's day; their value fell subsequently to £21; then recovered to £36. This illustrates the fact that Brighton, like most of southern England, enjoyed reasonable stability and hence prosperity during this period, unlike the north which William had ravaged with ferocious thoroughness in punishment for the rebellions of Earls Edwin and Morcar.

As was said earlier, Domesday mentions a church in Brighton. The oldest is St Nicholas', for centuries but now no longer the parish church. No one knows whether or not the church of 1086 was on the same site. Most of the present (much-restored) structure is fourteenth-century, although it houses a font of Caen stone—dating from the mid-twelfth century—that Pevsner calls 'the best piece of Norman carving in Sussex'. Its panels show the baptism of Christ, the Last Supper and scenes from the life of St Nicholas who—appropriately to Brighton—is the patron saint of mariners and travellers.

Brighton and other places much further afield benefited in Norman times from the influence of a great religious house, the Priory of St Pancras at Lewes, which William de Warenne and his wife Gundrada founded after visiting the celebrated Benedictine monastery at Cluny in France.*
The Cluniac Priory, some sad post-Reformation fragments of which still stand, became a famous centre of art and learning and some authorities (but not all) believe it was the monks of St Pancras who created the twelfth-century wall paintings which can be seen in the early Norman church at Coombes (on the road from Lancing College to Steyning) and in the Saxon church at Clayton (just the other side of the Downs on the road from Brighton to Hassocks). Either of these can give some impression of what the interior of St Nicholas' Church must have been like in Norman times, when vivid representations of Christ in glory and the judgement of the blessed and the damned were set around the walls to impress the Gospel message on a congregation that could neither read nor write and could not follow the words of the Latin Mass.

----

*The chapel (or chantry) of St Bartholomew, which stood in the centre of mediaeval Brighton, was a subsidiary of the Priory of St Pancras.

The hill on which St Nicholas' stands was nearly a quarter of a mile outside the confines of the mediaeval town. Whether or not the site was chosen because of an association with pre-Christian rituals, it could certainly be justified on practical grounds, arising from the fact that the close proximity of the south coast of England and the northern coast of France had made them—from the declining years of the Roman Empire onwards—convenient bases and tempting targets for seaborne raids.

It is necessary to explain at this point that mediaeval Brighton consisted almost entirely of a huddle of narrow alleys whose layout can still be followed in the old quarter of the town known as 'The Lanes' (a favourite loitering place for visitors). There were other streets south of these but they have long since disappeared under successive inundations of the sea. Although the Lanes retain something of their mediaeval aura, few of the houses belong to a period earlier than the eighteenth century and most are of the nineteenth.

Anyone determined to know what the original buildings were like should take the trouble of tracking down Brighton's oldest (and least-known) house.

Dating from the fifteenth century, it is in the former village (now suburb) of Moulsecoomb, two miles north of Brighton's sea-front, on the road to Lewes. In the shadow of the new College of Technology is an early nineteenth-century house of yellow brick called Moulsecoomb Place. Tucked away behind it, its existence unsuspected by many people who have lived in Brighton all their lives, is what Nikolaus Pevsner describes as 'the one and only worthwhile timber-framed cottage in Brighton'. When the Place was built the cottage became its stables and it is now used as an outbuilding by the Corporation's Parks and Gardens Department.

A closely packed maze of buildings like the Lanes would be a vulnerable and inflammable target for determined raiders and one can imagine the confusion as panic-stricken fugitives jammed the narrow streets. On such occasions the church, solidly built of stone, often served as an armoury and even as a fortress. In Brighton's case there was obvious virtue in siting such a building well on the landward side; in an open situation so that the inhabitants had a clear run to it; and on a hill so that its tower could serve as a look-out. (Today St Nicholas' still countrified churchyard is hemmed in with buildings, but as late as 1827 a French visitor reported standing there on a clear day and seeing the Isle of Wight, which is 60 miles away.)

It should, of course, be remembered that—except possibly for overseas expeditions—the distinction between soldier and civilian was not always easy to make; when there was danger of invasion every male could be called out with the 'shire levy', a mediaeval Home Guard. The Statute of Winchester (1285) even laid down what arms a man should bear, there being a sliding scale based on his annual income.

'Every man between 15 and 60 years of age', it said, 'shall be assessed and obliged to have arms according to the quantity of his lands and goods: that is, he who holds land worth over £15 a year, and goods worth 40 marks, shall have a coat of mail, an iron helmet, a sword, a knife, and a horse' and so on down to those who possessed 'goods worth less than 20 marks' who had to equip themselves with 'swords, knives and other smaller weapons'. As for those who were even poorer, they would carry bows and arrows.

As we shall see later, the inhabitants made effective use of their skill as bowmen as late as the sixteenth century, and the kings of England and their ministers were concerned that constant practice at the butts should maintain the national standard of markmanship.

It is from Edward III's reign and in the context of war with France that we have information that throws a brief light on the state of Brighton and its neighbours in the fourteenth century.

In 1337 Edward, afflicted with what Trevelyan calls 'the Plantagenet itch to conquer France', began the long-drawn-out conflict now known as the Hundred Years' War. For a foreign war professional soldiers were preferable to feudal levies, but professionals needed paying, so the king's ministers had to raise money by taxation.

In 1340, therefore, commissioners were appointed to levy the 'Nonae' or ninths; in other words the king was to claim every ninth lamb, ninth fleece and ninth sheaf of corn.

A similar 'inquisition' had been held half a century before to raise money for the Pope and nearly all the seaside parishes of Sussex were able to justify a reduced valuation in 1341 on the grounds that much former farmland had been inundated by the sea in the intervening period—possibly over 5,000 acres in the county as a whole. Brighton reported 'forty acres submerged for ever', Hove 'a hundred and fifty acres drowned by the sea' and Rottingdean 'fifty acres of arable land lost, destroyed and annihilated by the violence of the sea'.

But many other grounds were advanced for a reduced assessment. It was at Rottingdean that 240 acres of arable land were unsown because the peasants were too poor to buy seed, while in Brighton a drought had caused a failure of the wheat crop over 160 acres and a 'murrain' (infectious disease) among the sheep had caused fewer lambs to be born.

Ovingdean complained that a 100 acres of arable land were 'lying annihilated by the rabbits of Lord Earl Warenne'. (It was a frequent grievance of the peasantry that they had to provide free food for rabbits and pigeons that would eventually appear on the table of the manor. A dovecot built to accommodate some hundreds of birds can be seen at Patcham Court Farm, opposite Patcham Parish Church; there is another superb specimen at Newtimber Place on the other side of the Downs, near the village of Poynings.)

Many places—but not on this occasion Brighton—pleaded attacks by the enemy as the cause of their distress. Seaford, for example, ten miles east of Brighton and on flat, open ground between the mouths of the Ouse and the Cuckmere, could produce neither lambs nor fleeces because it had been repeatedly destroyed 'by divers assaults of our enemies from France and men of the parish bodily wounded and killed'.*

Rottingdean was attacked by the French in 1377, so successfully that they carried off for ransom the leaders of the force sent against them—the Prior of Lewes, two knights and a squire.

But there is no record of such an event at Brighton until the reign of Henry VIII. Whether there was one Brighton catastrophe or two has—for 100 years or more—provided the kind of debate historians most enjoy.

The debate centres round one of those maps decorated with drawings of ships and marching men that bring back nostalgic memories of the first time one read *Treasure Island*. The original is in the British Museum** and was reproduced in volume 24 of the periodical, *Archaeologia*, in 1832, when it was described as a 'Representation of the Attack made by the French Fleet upon Brighthelmstone, A.D. 1545.'

Short captions are written in at various points on the map to help the reader follow what is happening and more than one historian believes that the manner in which some of these are phrased gives a clear indication of its real purpose.

Brighton is shown as a small quadrangle of about 100 houses between two roads that run down to the beach from the Downs; while just to the west is the village of Hove—another 12 houses and a church. Brighton has a few houses on the beach (presumably survivors of the inundations) but all the rest are within an area bounded by what are now known as East

*W. H. Blaauw: *Remarks on the Nonae of 1340, as relating to Sussex* in *Sussex Archaeological Collections*, Vol. I (1847)
**Cotton MS., Aug. I, i, 18

Street, North Street and West Street. They are built round an open space, 'a felde in the middle of the town', usually called 'The Hempshares' because here was grown the hemp from which the fishermen made their nets. The north-west corner of the quadrangle is some way short of the church, reached by a track that winds up the hill.

The artist has been careful to show flames issuing from almost every house and a west wind is driving great billowing clouds of smoke across the scene.

Seven large men-of-war are apparently anchored close inshore, broadside on. Four others and three galleys, two of them with lateen sails, are a short distance offshore, presumably to guard against a surprise attack by the British fleet. Seven galleys have been beached and a large body of pikemen, with a banner, is marching from the the galleys towards the town.

Other armed men appear at several other points in the scene, but which are intended to be friends and which are foes no one has ever been able to say with any certainty.

A good deal of the written information is straightforwardly factual. For instance, on the top of a down just east of the road to Poynings is 'the bekon of the towne', depicted as flaming fiercely to alert the surrounding countryside to what is happening. And written across the beach where the Lewes road debouches are the words: 'Here landed the galeys'; while under the large sailing vessels is the caption: 'These grete Shippes ryding hardabord shore by shŏting into the hille and valeis over the towne, so sore oppresse the towne that the Countrey dare not adventure to reskue it', in other words by firing broadsides over the tops of the houses the warships are preventing any relieving force from reaching the town.

But others of the inscriptions strike a quite different note, apparently referring not to any specific raid but giving general information which could be useful at any time. Where the Poynings road joins the beach is written: 'Upon this west pte. may lond Cm p'sones unletted by any provision there'—Upon this west part may land 100,000 persons unhindered by any provision (i.e. any form of defence) there.

In similar vein are: 'The west part of Brithampton, all daungerous and without Cleves', presumably meaning that the absence of cliffs constitutes a danger because it is easy for troops to land and deploy; and 'Shippes may ride all somer w't'in di. a myle the towne in v. fathoms of water' (Ships may ride all summer within half (demi) a mile of the town in five fathoms of water).

Finally, in the top left-hand corner, in a noticeably different hand-writing, is the annotation which has been the hub of the controversy. It says: '1545 Iulye. 37. Hen, viij', i.e. '1545, July, in the 37th year of the reign of Henry the Eighth'.

Tudor chroniclers make two references to French hostile intentions against Brighton—one in June, 1514, the other in July, 1545.

Early in Henry VIII's reign, in accordance with Cardinal Wolsey's policy of 'balance of power', England began to make various interventions in Europe to ensure that neither France nor Spain should achieve so overwhelming an ascendancy as to dominate Europe—and so threaten England's safety.

In April 1513, the Lord High Admiral of England, Sir Edward Howard, lost his life in an ill-conceived and disastrous attack on a French fleet anchored at Brest under the command of Admiral Prégent (whose name was 'englished' into 'Prior John'). Two months later Prégent descended on the Sussex coast. This is how Edward Hall described the episode in his chronicle, 'The Union of the Noble and Illustre Families of Lancaster and York', first published in 1542:

'About this time, the warres yet contynewynge betwene England and Fraunce, Prior Jhon, great capitayne of the Frenche navy, with his galleys and foystes,* charged with great basylyskes and other greate artilery, came on the border of Sussex and came a-land in the night at a poore village called Bright Helmston, and, or the watch could him escrye, he sett fyer on the towne and toke suche poore goodes as he founde. Then the watch fyred the bekyns, and people began to gather; which seynge, Prior Jhon sowned his trompett to call his men aborde; and by that it was day. Then vi. archers which kept the watche folowed Prior Jhon to the sea and shott so fast that they bett the galeymen from the shore, and Prior Jhon hymselfe waded to his foyst, and th'Englishmen went into the water after, but they were put back with pickes, or els they had entered the foyst; but they shott so fast they wounded many in the foyst, and Prior Jhon was shott in the face with an arrow, and was like to have dyed. And therefore he offered his image of wax before Our Lady at Bolleyn [Boulogne] with the English arrow in the face for a myracle.'

---

*Light galleys.

No less than 21 towns and villages are said to have been destroyed in an English reprisal raid on the coast of Normandy led by Sir Edmund Howard's brother, Thomas; yet the kings of England and France had started to play quite a different game even before Brighton was attacked. Early in that year Henry decided that he was doing most of the fighting while his allies, the King of Spain and the Emperor Maximilian was reaping most of the benefits. So he decided to make a separate peace with France and a treaty was signed in July 1514—only a month after Brighton was burned to the ground.

Thirty years later Henry was again campaigning in France, although by now he was so diseased and so prematurely aged that he had to be carried everywhere on a litter. The English army's only significant achievement was to capture Boulogne. (Robert Baker, master of a 40-ton vessel, the *Trinity* of Brighthelmston, was among those who loaded a cargo of iron shot at the Tower of London and carried it across the Channel to be used in the bombardment of the besieged town.)

This time it was Henry's ally—Charles V, Emperor and King of Spain—who made a separate peace. But Henry was determined to keep Boulogne, so the war dragged on and a French fleet set off to neutralise the English navy before attempting to win back the town by a seaborne attack.

Raphael Holinshed relates what followed in his 'Chronicle' of 1578: 'in 37 Hen. VIII. 1545, July 18th, the Admiral of France, Monsr. Danebalte [Claude d'Annebaut], hoised up sailes, and with his whole Navy (which consisted of two hundred ships and twenty-six gallies) came forth into the seas, and arrived on the coast of Sussex before Bright Hamstead, and set certain of his soldiers on land to burn and spoil the country: but the beacons were fired, and the inhabitants thereabouts came down so thick, that the Frenchmen were driven to flie with loss of diverse of their numbers: so that they did little hurt there.'

After an abortive landing in the Isle of Wight, the French 'drew along the coast of Sussex, and a small number of them landed again in Sussex, of whom few returned to their ships; and for diverse gentlemen of the country, as Sir Nicholas Pelham and others, with such power as was raised upon the sudden, took them up by the way and quickly distressed them. When they had searched every where by the coast, and saw men still ready to receive them with battle, they turned stern, and so got them home again without any act achieved worthy to be mentioned'.

A paper read to the Royal Historical Society by Dr James Gairdner in

1906* points out that although the Privy Council papers of July 1545 include no less than four letters about a French landing at Seaford, they make no mention of the complete destruction of Brighton by fire—an event surely sufficiently serious not to have been ignored. Seaford, ten miles east of Brighton on level ground between the rivers Ouse and Cuckmere has no cliffs to making landing difficult, a feature of which a contemporary French writer on these events makes particular mention.

Martin du Bellay, a distinguished French soldier whose 'Memoirs' cover the period 1513 to 1547, is quoted by Dr Gairdner. He makes no mention of any French landing on the outward voyage but gives a detailed account of events occurring on the way home at a place which he calls 'Valseau' and locates fourteen 'leagues' east of the Isle of Wight.

The 'league' is a notoriously elastic measure, varying from one mile to five according to date and the nationality of the writer, but if one takes the commonest equivalent (3 miles) then du Bellay's 'Valseau' is at or very near Seaford, an identification strengthened by the fact that the 'deep tidal stream' which he mentions sounds very like the Ouse. Admittedly the place-name represents some difficulty because none of the villages on the lower reaches of the Ouse have (or had in 1545) a name even remotely resembling 'Valseau'. A possible explanation is that the 'Hundred' or county sub-division in which these villages are located was called 'Holmestrowe', which when spoken by a Sussex tongue into a French ear might register as 'Valseau' (a change no stranger than 'Wipers' for Ypres).

Here is the relevant passage from du Bellay which sounds as if it is based on an eye-witness account by one of the survivors: 'This place being level ground and open, seemed to our men so tempting that a good number took it into their heads to land there quite irregularly in the absence of their colonel; and, having got a little distance from the sea, they set upon an out-of-the-way village where they expected to make booty. But enemies were waiting for them near a deep tidal stream, who, seeing that some of our men had crossed on planks, suddenly rushed out from a little fort where they had lain hid, and after breaking the bridge to cut off the passage to the rest, attacked those on their side so vigorously as to compel them to save their lives by flight. But on re-crossing the stream some were carried away by the current and drowned. Others who could

---

*James Gairdner, LL.D, C.B.: *On a Contemporary Drawing of the Burning of Brighton in the Time of Henry VIII* (Transactions of the Royal Historical Society, 3rd Series, Vol. I, 1907)

swim battled with the torrent and saved themselves by the favour of their companions on the other bank, who protected them by shots of harquebuses.'

The English hero of this exploit was Sir Nicholas Pelham—an ancestor of the Earls of Chichester—whose punning epitaph is quoted at the head of this chapter. It is engraved on a fine monument of painted marble in the wall of the church of St Michael in Lewes High Street. He and his wife are shown kneeling on either side of a *prie-Dieu* while their ten children appear on a smaller scale beneath.

If there was no landing at Brighton in 1545 or, at most, one which 'did little hurt' what is the explanation of the sensational drawing? The theory has been advanced* (rightly, in my view) that it was part of a report by commissioners whom Henry appointed in 1539 to identify vulnerable points on the south coast and recommend measures for their reinforcement. One of the commissioners was Sir John Gage, of Firle (a manor near Lewes), who is known to have attended a meeting of the Privy Council which Henry held at Greenwich on 1 July, by which time it was known that a large French fleet had collected at Le Havre. A forceful way of underlining Brighton's insecurity would be a map incorporating a reminder of what had happened in 1514; what is more likely than that Sir John should have brought it up for discussion at that meeting?

The danger past the matter seems to have been shelved for it was not until the first year of Elizabeth's reign (1558) that 'there was granted to the inhabitants of that towne by the Lordes one parcell of land contayninge in length 30 feete & in bredth 16 feete, to keepe armor &c, nowe called the blockhouse'.

But even this left much to be desired and in 1587 when not a French but a Spanish invasion was threatened and only Drake's 'singeing of the King of Spain's beard' bought a year's breathing space, the two deputy-lieutenants of Sussex were directed to make a rapid survey of the coastal defences and reported as follows (demi-culverins, sacres, minions and falcons are all types of cannon):

'Betwene Brighthempston and Shoreham alongste the coaste is good landinge, for defence whereof yt were necessarie that ii dimyculverings and ii sacres were kepte in some good howse to be redie at sudden and in

---

*Alfred Anscombe: *Prégent de Bidoux's Raid in Sussex in 1514 and the Cotton MS. Aug. I. i, 18* (Transactions of the Royal Historical Society III, Vol. VIII, 1914)

sundrie places to be intrenched & aptly with sonken flankers for small shotte.

'Brighthempston towne may well be strengthened with like flankers there is one dimyculveringe iii sacres one minion and one fawcon mounted and furnished with shotte and wante powdre' [i.e. gunpowder needs to be supplied].*

In the event, when the Great Armada arrived, none of this defensive array had to be used. Paul Dunvan, describing the atmosphere of 1588 in his *Ancient and Modern History of Lewes and Brighthelmston* (published in 1795) struck an appropriate note of sturdy patriotism for a time when we were—yet once again—at war with France: 'With a determination of the most obstinate resistance, the shores of Sussex in general were lined by the people when this tremendous armament passed in their view, pursued by the light and expert navy of England; and the event has gloriously exemplified to admiring posterity the successful energy of patriotism against the colossal preparations and unwieldy malice of despots.'

---

*East Sussex County Council, Local History Research Unit No. 5: *Brighton in Tudor and Stuart Times* (1969)

CHAPTER FOUR

The Civil War and Charles II

'Within this marble monument doth lie
Approved Faith, Honour and Loyalty;
In this cold clay he hath ta'en up his station,
That once preserved the Church, the Crown, the Nation.
When Charles the Great was nothing but a breath,
This valiant soul stepp'd between him and death.'

Epitaph to Captain Nicholas Tettersall, 1674,
in St Nicholas' Churchyard, Brighton

Dickens, Thackeray, Arnold Bennett and Graham Greene have all written about Brighton (and found it a congenial place in which to write) but it is to the boot-and-saddle romances of Robert Louis Stevenson and John Buchan that one must look for fictional parallels to the most famous episode in the town's history—the escape of Charles II after the Battle of Worcester.

When the Civil War that was to cost Charles I his head broke out in 1642, Sussex was almost solidly for the Parliament side. The King had few supporters in the eastern half of the county and only the gentry rallied to his cause in the west. The Duke of Norfolk's castle at Arundel was taken by the Parliamentary forces in the first year of the war, re-captured in 1643 and lost again in 1644; and his lesser stronghold at Bramber was battered to pieces. But by and large Sussex was little touched by the war (there was even a neutralist, pacifist league of farmers who called themselves 'The Clubmen' and tried to deny recruits and money to both sides).

It was in any case a curiously mild revolution when it is compared with others in later centuries and other countries. There was no ferocity to compare with France's Reign of Terror, during the last seven weeks of which 1,400 people were sent to the guillotine in Paris alone. Supporters of the King often had to bankrupt themselves to pay the fines imposed on them by Parliament but at least they lived to fight and enjoy another day. One reason for this was that it was not a 'class' war. Although, in broad terms, the King drew his support from the gentry who had been country landowners for centuries and Parliament from townsmen who had made their money in commerce, protagonists of both causes were to be found in every station of society; sometimes within the same family; often in the same circle of friends—who remained friends even at the height of hostilities.

Colonel Herbert Morley, of Glynde, one of the most active Parliament men in Sussex, was able to write as follows to his friend, Sir William Campion, in command of the garrison holding Borstall House in Buckinghamshire for the King: 'Our old acquaintance needs no apology. All your Sussex friends are in health, and continue their worthy affections towards you, especially valewing your welfare with their owne.'

It was also, by the standards of later times, war on a very small scale. At Marston Moor, one of the biggest battles of the whole war, the total number of troops engaged, Royalist and Parliamentarian, was 43,000—almost exactly the number of *casualties* at Gettysburg.

It is amusing to note that both sides were equally annoyed at the lack of enthusiasm with which Sussex men espoused either cause. Charles Thomas-Stanford, sometime Mayor and M.P. for Brighton, whose *Sussex in the Great Civil War and the Interregnum, 1642–1660*, (published in 1910) combines careful research and eminent readability in a way that puts it in the first rank of local histories, comments on the frequent appearance in the county of 'the "neuter", the moderate man, who was not a partisan, but for the sake of peace was ready to shout with the side that was uppermost . . . '.

This, then, was the background against which the events now to be described took place—two and a half years after Charles I's execution, when his son, Charles II, was on the run following a crushing defeat at the Battle of Worcester on 3 September 1651.

As soon as one reads the words 'Charles the Second', one is tempted to visualise the King as he appeared in portraits after the Restoration; splendid in wig, velvet and lace, observing the world with the humorous cynicism of maturity through those heavy-lidded eyes. But we are not concerned here with the Merry Monarch but with a tired, shabby young man of 21 who had known nothing but war and its nomad shifts since he was 12 years old and now had a price of £1,000 on his head in a part of the country not unduly favourable to his cause. To help disguise his identity he had sacrificed his cavalier curls after Worcester and now, with his pudding-basin haircut, dark clothes and steeple-crowned hat was—as he had hoped—taken by many of those he met to be a Puritan.

Samuel Pepys confessed to his diary that 'it made me ready to weep to hear the stories that he told of his difficulties that he had passed through; as his travelling for four days and nights on foot, every step up to his knees in dirt, with nothing but a green coat and a pair of country breeches on, and a pair of country shoes that made him so sore all over his feet that he could scarce stir.'

Yet through it all it is clear that, even at this age, Charles already possessed the insouciance that speaks to one from his later portraits and the cool head that was to keep him for 25 years on the throne that his brother lost in three. For details of this odyssey of escape we rely mainly on two accounts that have come down to us from Charles's day.

The first is Charles's own, taken down in shorthand by Mr Pepys in two lengthy sessions in October, 1680, and later transcribed in a manuscript which is now in the library of Magdalene College, Cambridge. Usually historians have grave reservations about the reliability of accounts set down many years—in this case 29 years—after the events they describe, but there is a convincing circumstantiality about this document, and various annotations and amendments bear witness to the care the king took to ensure its accuracy.

Moreover, in the relevant portions, there is close agreement with the other main manuscript source. This, now housed in the British Museum, is entitled:

'The last act, in the miraculous Storie of his Mties escape; being a true and perfect relation of his conveyance, through many dangers to a safe harbour; out of the reach of his tyrannical enemies; by Colonel Gounter; of Rackton in Sussex; who had the happiness to bee instrumental in the business, (as it was taken from his mouth by a person of worth a little before his death).'

Apparently Gounter or some member of his immediate family hid the document in the secret drawer of a cabinet and then forgot to pass on the fact of its existence for, when Racton House was dismantled in 1830, his descendants sold the cabinet to a Mr Bartlett, of Havant. He it was who found the secret spring and sold the manuscript to the British Museum in 1832.

For the first part of Charles's journey after Worcester we have to rely on his own story. He was determined to escape either to France or to Spain and his first thought was to embark from Bristol, but no suitable ship was sailing from there for a month.

With his hair cut short and disguised as a servant 'in a kind of grey cloth suit', Charles lay up for a time at Trent near Sherborne, in Dorset, where plans were put in hand for him to take ship to France from the little port of Lyme. These fell through—in a manner that Charles and his companions were to bear ruefully in mind when similar plans were laid in Brighton. Although the ship's captain had not confided in his wife, she guessed who his mysterious passenger was to be and, with the help of her two daughters, kept him locked in his room until the ship had missed the tide.

Attempts to embark from Southampton also failed; the only available vessel was requisitioned by the Government to transport troops to Jersey!

So Charles began his travels once more, passing through Stonehenge where (with characteristic *sangfroid*) he 'stayed looking upon the stones some time' and spending four or five days in a priest's hole—'a hiding hole that was very convenient and safe'—at Heale House near Salisbury.

It was at this time that Lord Wilmot, who had been continuously active on Charles's behalf, found a promising contact in Colonel George Gounter, 'a most prudent and loyal gentleman', of Racton House, near Chichester. Returning home on the night of 7 October, Gounter found his wife sitting by the fire with a so-called 'Devonshire gentleman . . . by name Mr Barlowe', whom he recognised as Lord Wilmot.

On tenterhooks to know what could have brought Wilmot to his house under an assumed name, the Colonel eventually got him alone, when Wilmot asked his help in finding a ship for 'the King of England, my maister, your maister, and the maister of all good Englishmen'. This Gounter undertook to do 'with all possible care and alacritie', whereupon 'the noble lord . . . was abundantly satisfied with his answer, hugging him in his armes, and kissed his cheeks againe and againe'.

Then for the second time in this chapter of Charles's life, we come across an inquisitive wife, determined that her husband shall have no secrets from her. The Colonel's story continues with a scene common to all periods of history: the bedtime inquisition.

'Coming into his chamber, he found his wife had stayed up for him, and was earnest to know whoe this was, and what was his business. The Coll. desired her to excuse him, assuring her it was nothing concerning her, or, that would in any wayes damnifye her. Shee was confident that there was more in it than soe, and enough shee doubted, to ruine him, and all his family; and in that, said shee, I am concerned; breaking out into a very great passion of weeping.

'Which the Coll. seeing, took a candle and pretending to goe into the next roome, but privatly to my Lord Wilmot, and acquainted him how it was; asking his advice, whether, as the case stood, it were any way amisse, to acquaint her with it. That he durst pass his word, for the loyaltie and integritie of his wife: however without his allowance [permission] she would knowe nothing. The Noble Lord replied: No, no, by all means acquaint her with it.

'He humbly thancked him, and badd him good night againe. The Col. coming into his chamber unfolded the busines, wyped the teares of his ladyes eyes, whoe smiling, said, Goe on, and prosper.'

First enquiries were fruitless but eventually Gounter heard of a Mr Francis Mancell, a merchant, 'one that usually traded into France'.

'He [Mancell] received him courteously, and entertained him with a bottle or twoe of his French wine, and Spanish tobacco. After a whyle the Coll. broke the business to him, saying, I doe not only come to visitt you, but must request one favour of you. He replied: Any thing in his power. Then the Coll. asked him, if he could fraught a bark [charter a ship]; for, he said, I have twoe speciall friends of mine that have been engaged in a duell, and there is mischief done, and I am obliged to get them of [off] if I can. Hee doubted not butt he could att such a place, att Brighthelmston in Sussex.'

By Saturday, 11 October, all was agreed. The captain of the ship was 'to bee in readiness upon an howers warning; and the merchant to stay there, under the pretence of fraughting his bark; to see all in readiness against the Coll. and his twoe friends arrival.' Mancell was to receive £50 'for his paines' and the ship's master, Nicholas Tettersall (whom Gounter calls Tettersfield) £60.

On Monday the 13th the Colonel, his cousin and Lord Wilmot, with two greyhounds trotting beside them to give colour to the pretence that they were coursing hares, rendezvoused with the King and Robin Philips on a hill called Old Winchester above the village of Warnford. That night they all lodged at the house of the Gounters' sister, Mrs Symonds, at Hambledon, seven miles from Portsmouth.

The King slept well, Gounter tells us, and by dawn they were on their way, the Colonel pocketing a couple of ox-tongues 'which he thought they might need'. Near Arundel Castle they ran full tilt into the Parlia-

mentarian governor, but he and his escort galloped past, paying no attention to the group who moved respectfully to the side of the road. ('The
King beeing told who it was, replied merrily, I did not like his starched
mouchates [moustaches].'

In the nearby village of Houghton they stopped briefly at the George
and Dragon inn to buy bread and beer which they ate with their ox-
tongues.

Crossing the Arun by the old stone bridge they took the steep chalk
track up to Amberley Mount and rode along the ridge of the Downs,
descending into the gap where the village of Washington stands and then
climbing again to Chanctonbury Ring (still treeless at this date). Again
they followed the downland track which, because of its openness and the
fall of the land on either side would give them early warning of any body of
pursuers moving to intercept them.

Curving down into the valley of the Adur at the village of Bramber
(where the ruins of the castle destroyed during the Civil War can still be
seen) they found the streets full of Parliament soldiers. Wilmot wanted to
turn back, but the King and Gounter agreed they should 'goe on boldly'
and so they 'passed through, without any hinderance'.

The little village of Beeding lay next on their road and here the party
decided to split up for the time being. Gounter wanted the King to spend
the night there while he reconnoitred the coast.

Gounter continues: 'But my Lord Wilmot would by noe means for feare
of those soldiers, but carried the king out of the road I know not whither.
Soe we parted; they where they thought safest, I to Brightemston; being
agreed they should send to me, when fixed anywhere and ready.'

Neither document is specific about the routes taken, but it is generally
assumed that Gounter went by the direct road to Shoreham and then
along what is now called the 'Old Shoreham Road' into Brighton; while
the King and Wilmot took the less-frequented track past the motte-
and-bailey on Edburton Hill and the Devil's Dyke and thence into the
town by way of the Dyke Road.

This would make sense in view of Gounter's desire to delay entering
Brighton 'till he had viewed the coast' and Lord Wilmot's insistence that
he should carry the King 'out of the road' for fear of the soldiers.

They all met safely at the George inn in Brighton. (It no longer exists
but historians still argue whether it stood in West Street or Middle Street.
It was probably very like the George and Dragon at Houghton, which has
been little changed since Charles's day.)

'At supper', says Gounter, 'the king was cheerful, not shewing the least signe of feare, or apprehension of any daunger; neither then, nor att any tyme during the whole course of this busines. Which is noe small wonder, considering that the very thought of his ennemies, soe great and soe many, soe diligent and soe much interested in his ruine, was enough, as long as he was within their reach and, as it were, in the very middest of them, to have daunted the stoutest courage in the world.'

At this late stage, with his ship only awaiting the tide to float it off the beach, Charles was twice recognised, according to his own account. The innkeeper himself, said Charles, 'came in and fell a talking with me, and just as he was looking about and saw there was nobody in the room, he upon a sudden kissed my hand that was on the back of the chair and said to me, God bless you, wheresoever you go, I doubt not before I die but to be a lord, and my wife a lady; so I laughed and went away into the next room, not desiring then any further discourse with him there being no remedy against my being known by him, and more discourse might have raised suspicion, on which consideration I thought it best to trust him in the matter; and he proved honest.'

He told Gounter that the innkeeper was 'one . . . that belonged to the back staires to my Father', presumably meaning he was a servant at the Palace in Whitehall.

By an almost incredible coincidence the captain of the ship on which he was to travel, Nicholas Tettersall, had also met the King before.

'I observed that the master of the vessel looked very hard on me', says the King in Pepys MS., 'and as soon as we had supped called the merchant aside and the master told him that he had not dealt fair with him, for though he had given him a very good price for carrying over that gentleman, yet he had not been clear with him; for (says he) he is the king, as I very well know him to be so; upon which, the merchant denying it, saying that he was mistaken, the master answered I know him very well, for he took my ship, together with other fishing vessels at Brighthelmstone in the year 1648—which was when I commanded the king, my father's fleet; and I very kindly let them go again. But (says he) be not troubled at it, for I think I do my God and my country good service in preserving the king, and by the grace of God I will venture my life and all for him and set him safe on shore, if I can, in France.'

When Mancell told Charles of this, the King remembered the ship's captain in Dorset whose wife had barricaded him into his room. 'Thinking it convenient not to let him go home, lest he should be asking advice of his wife, or any one else, we kept him in the inn, and sat up all night drinking beer and taking tobacco with him.'

The two accounts differ a little at this point because Gounter claims that he eventually 'perswaded the king to take some rest' in the early hours of the morning, when Tettersall was allowed to leave 'to provide for necessaries' (which could mean any number of things). More surprisingly he says nothing of Tettersall's discovery of the King's identity; but he does describe some last-minute hard bargaining by the captain who—if he had recognised Charles—was certainly the man to exploit his knowledge. Gounter and the King finally succumbed to his insistence that, in addition to the terms already agreed, they should insure his vessel for £200.

At four o'clock in the morning horses were brought to the back door of the inn and they all rode to a spot between Brighton and Shoreham where the 40-ton coal-brig, the *Surprise*, lay beached.

Here Tettersall thought it necessary to renew his protestations of disinterested loyalty. 'I was no sooner got into the ship and lay down upon the bed', says Charles, 'but the master came in to me, fell down on his knees and kissed my hand, telling me that he knew me very well, and that he would venture life and all he had in the world, to set me safe down in France.'

Gounter was still standing patiently by with the horses 'in case anything unexpected happened'. The brig was lifted off by the tide at seven but it was afternoon before it was lost to Gounter's view and he started for home. (Two hours later a troop of Parliament cavalry trotted into Brighton, looking for 'a tall black man 6 foot and 4 inches high'.)

Meanwhile, on board the *Surprise*, Captain Tettersall—most circumspect of heroes—was taking out yet more 'insurance', designed this time to establish his innocence should they be intercepted and Charles taken prisoner.

Charles, clearly amused by Tettersall, told Pepys how carefully this grubby Machiavelli hedged his bets: 'We went out of port, but the master being bound for Pool [i.e. Poole, in Dorset], laden with sea-coal, because he would not have it seen from Shoreham that he did not go his intended voyage, but stood all day with a very easy sail towards the Isle of Wight, only my Lord Wilmot and myself of my company on board, and as we were sailing, the master came to me, and desired me to persuade his men to use their endeavour (with me) to get him to set us ashore in France, the better to cover him from any suspicion thereof, upon which I sent to the men, which were four and a boy, and told them truly that we were two merchants that had some misfortunes, and were a little in debt; that we had some money owing to us in Rouen, in France, and were afraid of being arrested in England; that if they would persuade the master (the wind being very fair) to give us a trip over to Dieppe, or one of the ports near Rouen, they would oblige us very much; and with that I gave them twenty shillings to drink, upon which they undertook to second me if I were to propose it to their master. So I went to the master and told him our condition, and that if he would give us a trip over to France, we would give him a consideration for it; upon which he counterfeited a difficulty, saying it would hinder his voyage, but his men, as they had promised, joined their persuasions to ours, and at last he yielded to set us over.'

So they set course for France, making a landfall at 'Feckham' (Fécamp) where Charles and Lord Wilmot were set ashore in a small boat. Three days later they had joined the Queen Mother in Paris.

Some accounts of Brighton's history jump forward from this event to the Restoration when Mancell, Colonel Gounter's widow and Tettersall all (after a certain number of pressing reminders) received pensions from the King. Tettersall in particular—it is his self-congratulatory epitaph which heads this chapter—set in train a rise in his family's fortunes by his part in the Royal escape. His great-great-great grandson became a knight and *his* daughter married a baronet, Sir George Shiffner, of Lewes.

But in fact a number of fascinating political convolutions took place in this part of Sussex between Charles's flight and his triumphant return in 1660. Two places associated with these episodes are now inside Brighton's boundaries although they were distinct and separate from it in the seventeenth century.

The first is Patcham Place,* which lies on the right, partly hidden by trees, as one enters the village of Patcham on the road from London. It is sometimes referred to mistakenly as an eighteenth-century mansion. This is the date of the 'mathematical tiles' which are its distinctive feature. These look like neat, shiny black bricks but are in fact L-shaped tiles hung on a wooden frame or rack that forms a false façade to the original, Tudor walls of flint-and-rubble.

Patcham Place was bought in about 1615 by Anthony Stapley, who subsequently became a prominent supporter of the Parliamentary cause and was one of those who signed Charles I's death-warrant—in this house, according to local tradition (which also says his remorseful spirit still haunts it).

*Now a youth hostel.

open arms and 'wished more such good men would come over'. They
stayed for a time at Cambridge, holding meetings at which 'they preached
and prayed and were looked upon as men dropped from Heaven'. Early in
the following year two King's men arrived from England to arrest them.
Governor Endicott put up a pretence of co-operation but in fact no one in
the colony showed any inclination to help in the capture of the fugitives.
They lived in hiding for three years until the hue-and-cry died down; for
part of the time in a cave in woods near Newhaven, Massachusetts, at a
place to which—like characters from *Pilgrim's Progress*—they gave the
name of 'Providence Hill'.

In 1664 they moved on to Hadley where they lived with a Rev. John
Russell and in 1675 Goffe, the Civil War veteran, put his military talents
at the service of his American protectors. In that year the settlement was
attacked by Indians and it was Goffe's leadership that saved it from destruction. His last letter to his family in England was dated 2 April 1679, so
it is presumed that he died in that year.

Anyone who wishes to catch the true flavour of this period cannot do
better than to visit Danny, a lovely country house tucked under the northern slope of Wolstenbury Hill, a mile south of Hurstpierpoint.

A Tudor House with some early eighteenth-century additions, it
epitomises the indestructability of the English country gentry in the face
of civil strife and political earthquakes. It still belongs to descendants of
Sir William Campion,* the cavalier whom we met earlier in this chapter,
and the family tree also includes the Royalist Gorings; a Kentish family of
Parliament sympathies, the Courthopes; and the weathercock Stapleys.
The magnificent parade of ancestral portraits alone justifies a visit.

---

*Although leased to the Mutual Householders Association, Ltd, which provides unfurnished accom-
tŏdation for retired professional people.

CHAPTER FIVE

Dr Russell's Cure for Eighteenth-Century Brighton

' . . . Brighthelmstone was only a small obscure village, occupied by fishermen, till silken Folly and bloated Disease, under the auspices of a Dr Russell, deemed it necessary to crowd one shore and fill the inhabitants with contempt for their visitors.'

Peregrine Phillips, *Bew's Diary* (1780)

For the past 200 years Brighton has been a Micawber among towns. Whenever decline and penury have threatened, something has turned up. But from the middle of the seventeenth to the middle of the eighteenth century its prosperity declined so noticeably that the gloomier prophets thought it would disappear altogether.

Even in Elizabeth's reign economics had begun to be a matter of concern to the inhabitants. In 1579 the fishermen of Brighton thought they were bearing an unfair proportion of the cost of the military defence of the town compared with the landsmen, the 'husbandmen and artificers'. The crews of fishing boats at that time were not paid wages, but shares in the proceeds of the catch, these shares being calculated according to certain traditional procedures. A quarter of one share was paid to the churchwardens for the upkeep of the church and for the defence of the locality against foreign raiders, but the fishermen thought they had a grievance—alleging that the landsmen were not taxed *pro rata*.

They said so in a petition to the Privy Council who, in the year following, appointed a distinguished four-man commission to look into the matter. It was headed by Lord Buckhurst, second cousin of the Queen and joint Lord-Lieutenant of the county. The other members were the Earl of Arundel, who held some of the de Warenne land in the Brighton area; Sir Thomas Shirley of Wiston (near Steyning); and Richard Shelley, whose family had Patcham Place before the Stapleys.

50

To avoid future misunderstandings the Commissioners decided 'to will and commande certeyne of the said auncient ffishermen to sett down in Wryting their auncient customs and orders concerninge the makinge payment and imployinge of the said Quarter share;* which having been done, the Commissioners stipulated the sums the landsmen had to pay, expressing the hope that this would serve 'ye better encrease of Amitye & neighbolye frendshippe among the said parties'.

This was a time of comparative well-being in Brighton for, as the record of the commission's findings says, the town had 80 fishing boats, 400 able seamen and 10,000 fishing nets. But inflation of prices was beginning to be a worry. The price of wood for instance—because the Sussex iron industry was consuming the forests of the Weald—had risen in a few years 'from three shillings and fower pence a tonn to thirteen shillings fower pence . . . '.

Thirty years later domestic and foreign interference was damaging the fishermen's prosperity and in 1609 they presented two petitions to Parliament.**

One of the best fishing grounds of their herring fleet was off the coast of East Anglia and the people of Yarmouth, resenting the competition of Brighton men selling their catches in what they regarded as their private territory, used various methods of harassment, described in the first petition as 'seizing upon their boats, imprisoning of their men, imposing great fines upon them, and hindering of them from fishing, to the loss of £200 in one night to them, the inhabitants of Brighthelmston . . . '

The second petition complained of interference by 'Dunkirks', that is, privateers sailing out of Dunkirk (then part of the Spanish Netherlands), 'whoe doe usually frequent the coaste wher they were wonte to fysh, and who having already taken one of their poore neighbours and made prize of his goodes, they do also fear to fall into their handes'.

The Civil War was to make matters even worse and yet another petition to Parliament in 1652 (there must have been a rich crop of village Hampdens in seventeenth-century Brighton) alleged that the fishermen 'by the force and rage of their enemies, the Dunkerks and French men of war . . . have been debarred of their former fishing voyages, and the sea hath been shut up from them, so that they could not go about their former

---

*Charles Webb and A. E. Wilson: *Elizabethan Brighton—The Ancient Customs of Brighthelmston 1580* (John Beal & Son Ltd, Brighton, 1952)
**The quotations from this point on until the first reference to Daniel Defoe are taken from *Brighton in Tudor and Stuart Times*, produced by Local History Research Unit No. 5 (East Sussex County Council, 1969)

affairs and have been hindered to the value of £30,000 . . . '

But the forces of nature did more harm to Brighton than any men-of-war. The encroachments of the sea which we have already noticed in Edward III's reign became increasingly menacing as more and more of the shingle beaches and the chalk cliffs was eroded and more of the buildings in the lower half of the town were swept away. A list made in 1665 of premises in the lower town that paid rent to the Lord of the Manor bears a note that 'previous to 1665' (it does not say *from* what date) the sea had destroyed 22 properties below the cliffs, including 12 shops and three cottages. But there still remained 113 'tenements' some of which were only 'capstan-places' and others probably no more than rough sheds for storing nets and tackle.

Eleven years later William Jeffery, yeoman, of Brighton, went before the Justices of the Peace at Lewes and deposed in open court that 'in case there be not a peere [pier] or some other speedy course taken for the security of the sd [said] port all or the most parte of the said Towne and p'ish [parish] of Brighthelmston will be in danger of being swallowed up by the raging of the sea The charge of wch [which] peer or other security to the port will amount to the sume of 7000£ att the least'.

What did Jefferys' '£7,000' represent in real terms at that period, compared with our concept of such a sum? One can best arrive at an answer that has meaning for a twentieth-century reader by relating it to the amount of money on which a family had to live at this date.

Fortunately figures applicable to the year 1688 were compiled by a certain Gregory King (who, in addition to being a statistician, was an engraver, a genealogist and a herald).* He calculated that £6. 10s. was needed to keep a pauper, his wife and one or two children alive—for a year. (About one-fifth of the population—over a million people—were, at this time, receiving their income from public relief funds for all or part of the year.)

The annual income of a labouring man or of a servant, not living in his employer's house and with a family of similar size to support, was about £15. An artisan would have £38; a farmer £42. 10s.; a shopkeeper, £45; and a person 'in liberal arts and sciences', £60. Those categorised as 'gentlemen' could keep up appearances on £280 per annum and at the top of the scale were the 'temporal lords' with £3,200 (spiritual lords gave most humble and hearty thanks for a mere £1,300).

---

*Gregory's table is given in full in G. M. Trevelyan's *English Social History* (Pelican, 1972)

So William Jefferys was advocating an expenditure which by our standard would be something like £1½ million; and the 'peer or other security' was almost certainly never built. In any case there was no improvement in Brighton's fortunes for in 1689 there was yet another appeal to the Lewes Justices, this time by the churchwardens and 'overseers of the poor', who declared that the cost of relieving and maintaining the poor of their parish had become 'soe greate and burdensome' that they could no longer bear it unless help was forthcoming from adjoining parishes which had few poor or none at all.

But these misfortunes were as nothing to those caused by the two great storms of 1703 and 1705. The first of these is movingly described in a pamphlet of which the editor was Daniel Defoe, the author of *Robinson Crusoe*. In this work, which he entitled *The Storm: or a Collection of the most Remarkable Casualties and Disasters which happen'd in the Late Dreadful Tempest both by Sea and Land*, he collected together eye-witness accounts of the event provided by some dozens of local correspondents all over the country.

This is the 'melancholy account' he received from Brighton:
'The late dreadful tempest in November 27, 1703, last, had very terrible effects in this town. It began here much about one of the clock in the morning, the violence of the wind stript a great many houses, turn'd up the leads off the church, overthrew two windmills, and laid them flat on the ground, the town in general (upon the approach of daylight) looking as if it had been bombarded. Several vessels belonging to this town were lost, others stranded, and driven ashoar, others forced over to Holland and Hamborough (Hamburg), to the great impoverishment of the place. Derick Pain, Junior, master of the Elizabeth ketch of this town lost, with all his company. George Taylor, master of the ketch call'd the Happy Entrance, lost, and his company, excepting Walter Street, who swimming three days on a mast between the Downs and North Yarmouth, was at last taken up. Richard Webb, master of the ketch call'd the Richard and Rose, of Brighthelmston, lost, and all his company, near St. Hellens. Edward Friend, master of the ketch called Thomas and Francis, stranded near Portsmouth. Edward Glover, master of the pink* call'd Richard and Benjamin, stranded near Chichester, lost one of his men, and he, and the rest of his company, forced to hang in the shrouds several hours. George Beach, junior, master of the pink call'd

---

*A small, flat-bottomed boat of a design that probably originated in Holland.

Mary, driven over to Hamborough from the Downes, having lost his anchor, cables and sails. Robert Kichener, master of the Cholmley pink of Brighton, lost near the Roseant with nine men, five men and a boy saved by another vessel. This is all out of this town, beside the loss of several other able seamen belonging to this place, aboard of her Majesty's ships, transports and tenders.'

A second storm, two years later, completed the destruction of the buildings on the beach—so that even their sites were hidden under several feet of shingle—as well as severely damaging several of the newly repaired houses in the upper town.

It was not long after this that Defoe wrote another book which, though less acclaimed than his novels, has been well regarded by generations of historians as a valuable piece of contemporary reporting, despite the fact that—like *The Storm*—it probably contains much material that the author obtained at second-hand rather than by personal observation.

A Tour Through the Whole Island of Great Britain contains two sentences that present a most dismal picture of contemporary Brighton and writers on the town's history have hitherto confined themselves to quoting these. There is, however, a second passage which modifies very considerably the pessimistic tone of the first.

The earlier reference is worth quoting in context because it helps us to see Brighton in the setting of its time, reminding us that at the beginning of the eighteenth century it was only a dowdy unconsidered neighbour of the genteel and prosperous county town:

'Lewis (Lewes) is a fine pleasant town, well built, agreeably situated in the middle of an open champaign country, and on the edge of the South Downs, the pleasantest and most delightful of their kind in the nation. . . . From this town, following still the range of the South Downs, west, we ride in view of the sea, and on a fine carpet ground for about twelve miles to Bright Helmston, commonly called Bredhemston,* a poor fishing town, old built, and on the very edge of the sea. The sea is very unkind to this town, and has by its continual encroachments, so gained upon them, that in a little more they might reasonably expect it would eat up the whole town, above 100 houses having been devoured by the water in a few years past; they are now obliged to get a brief

---

*An accurately phonetic rendering of broad Sussex speech—Author

granted them, to beg money all over England, to raise banks against the water; the expense of which, the brief expressly says, will be eight thousand pounds which if one were to look on the town, would seem to be more than all the houses in it are worth.'

(It was in 1722 that Brighton was granted a 'Church Brief', sometimes called a 'King's Letter', issued by the Sovereign as Head of the Church, to authorise a collection in churches throughout England in aid of some specific charitable object—in this case the erection of groynes to protect the town from further inundation.)

It is usually overlooked that the *Tour* has a second reference to Brighton, placing it in a list of important shipyards that includes places like Newcastle, Hull, Whitby, Portsmouth, Plymouth and Southampton.

Another item of information that does not altogether fit the picture of a town on the verge of extinction is a list of Sussex sailing vessels compiled in 1701 by the Commissioners of Customs for the Navy Board who (yet another war with the French being in prospect) wanted to know just how much merchant shipping was available. There was no system of port registration at this date, but vessels nevertheless had a base of operations which was generally acknowledged and, for 77 vessels out of the county total of 154, this was Brighton; and they accounted for 4,185 of the total tonnage of 6,919.

Nevertheless the 1730 edition of a national survey called *Magna Britannia* struck the same note as Defoe, asserting that 90 years before Brighton had been a flourishing town of 500 families, but added ominously that 'if some speedy Care be not taken to stop the Encroachments of the Ocean, it is probable the Town will in a few years be utterly depopulated; the Inhabitants being already diminished one-third less than they were, and those that remain are many of them Widows, Orphans, decrepid persons, and all very poor; insomuch that the Rates for their Relief are at the Rack-Rent. [i.e. extortionate level] of 8d in the Pound . . .'

A local historian, John George Bishop, published a book in 1895* which demonstrated what illuminating facts can be excavated from unpromising deposits. When the Guardians of the Poor moved their offices in the 1890's there came to light the 'Poor Rate Book' for the years 1744–1761, and from this Bishop was able to reconstruct to a considerable extent the layout of the town in 1744; to identify the names of families liv-

---

*J. G. Bishop: *Peeps into the Past: Brighton in 1744–1761 (Brighton Herald, 1895)*

ing there at that date; and to arrive at an estimate of population, for a period when there was no Government census to give accurate figures. He did this by taking the number of houses, 454, and multiplying it by 3½ to give a total of 1,589. (For the eighteenth century five might be a better figure for the number of people per household in a town like Brighton—which would give a population of 2,270.)

Such calculations will always be a matter of argument, but one firm fact emerges: three-quarters of the 454 households were so poverty-stricken that they were exempted from paying any rates at all.

Valuable though this pioneer work of Bishop's was, it is a piece of more recent research that has gone some way towards reconciling the apparent contradictions of earlier evidence and now enables us to form a much clearer picture of what it was like to live in Brighton in the first half of the eighteenth century.

It was to examine this period that a 'History of Brighton Project' was sponsored by the University of Sussex Centre for Continuing Education and began work (at the Friends' Centre in Brighton) in September, 1975.* The tutors, Sue and John Farrant, suggested to the part-time students that there was a rich vein of source-material still unworked. This was to be found in the parish registers of St Nicholas' Church and (at the East Sussex Record Office in Lewes) in wills and 'inventories'—that is, the lists of goods and chattels belonging to a dead man or woman that had to be prepared if the terms of the will were to be executed accurately and fairly.

Their expectations were justified. From these manuscripts (sometimes crabbed, but often copper-plate and reasonably easy to read once such idiosyncracies as phonetic spelling and the reversed 'e' were recognised) emerged a mass of fascinating data on everyday living during the years that had hitherto been considered almost totally devoid of interest—a sad interregnum between the hurried departure of Charles II and the more calculated arrival of the apocalyptic Dr Russell. Brighton was far from being the Deserted Village that Defoe and others had seemed to suggest.

Admittedly some of the material is tantalising in its brevity, the more so that further research is unlikely to throw further light on the events or people described. One such instance is dated 5 November 1708, in the parish register: 'Henry Back was buried who fell into a furnace of boiling liquor as he was brewing and livd twelve hours afterwards'. And there are

*J. H. & S. P. Farrant and contributors: *Brighton Before Dr Russell—An Interim Report* (Centre for Continuing Education, University of Sussex, 1976)

entries like that of 'Elizabeth daughter of JohnWeymark *buried poor*' and 'Anne Hartley a dumb maid' or 'John Kennet a stranger', 'Judith Brown a criple' and 'Derrie Pain, an antient man', curiously evocative because this is all we shall ever know about them.

The register of burials and the inventories together provide a cross-section of the trades carried on in the town at this period. Naturally there were mariners and farmers, but also shipwrights and ship's carpenters, house carpenters and bricklayers, millers, innkeepers, blacksmiths, malt-sters, sawyers, masons, tailors, shoemakers, an apothecary and an instrument-maker (who seemed to specialise in hour-glasses).

The marriage entries show—as one might expect in an age when roads where notoriously bad—that in most cases both bride and bridegroom were 'of this town', but occasional bridegrooms were recorded whose home parishes were Greenwich and Stepney, Rochester and the Isle of Wight, underlining the fact that Brighton vessels carried cargoes to and from the Thames and the Medway and all along the South Coast and no doubt recruited in these 'foreign' ports if they lost a man on the outward voyage.

Most revealing of the place and time are the inventories, which even tell us something of the way the average eighteenth-century resident spoke. This is because most of the spelling was by ear (and sometimes only understandable to a modern reader if spoken aloud a time or two). Thus 'too chayers' are 'two chairs', 'tubes' are 'tubs' and a 'screetore' is an 'escritoire'. There are traps to watch for. References to a 'larder' in fact concern a ladder, this pronunciation being one recorded by the Rev. W. D. Parish, vicar of Selmeston, in his *Dictionary of the Sussex Dialect* over a century later.*

Remembering that inventories were only taken when the deceased had property worth £5 or more (so that we are only meeting the more pros-perous), some of the inhabitants had astonishingly few possessions—astonishingly few, that is, by the (possibly transitory) standards of present-day Europe and North America. In one of his volumes of auto-biography** Leonard Woolf reminds us how bare a working man's home could be before the welfare state and the supermarket; even as late as World War I, which is the period he is describing. When he and Virginia Woolf were living in the country just outside Lewes, a local shepherd's

*Rev. W. D. Parish: *A Dictionary of the Sussex Dialect and Collection of Provincialisms in use in the County of Sussex*, edited in modern edition by Helena Hall (R. J. Acford, 1957)
**Leonard Woolf: *Beginning Again* (Hogarth Press, 1972)

wife 'did' for them. One evening she knocked at their door to tell them her daughter was giving birth to an illegitimate child and that she could not get a doctor. 'So bare was the home of a Sussex shepherd fifty years ago', Woolf explains, 'that she had not the necessary towels, basins, cans and she had to come to borrow them from us.'

But, to return to the eighteenth century, here is the list of the possessions of Widow Cobby; a very short list despite the fact that—having a small share in the ownership of a fishing boat—she was presumably better off than many of her neighbours:

'*A True Inventory* of all and
Singular the Goods, Chattells and Credites of Mary
Cobby late of Brighthelmstone in the County of Sussex
widow deceased *Taken and Appraised* by us whose
names are subscribed the Fourteenth day of March
Anno q. Dni 1717/18.*

	£. s. d.
Imprimis her wearing Apparel & money in Purss	01 : 10 : 00.
Item One Two and Thirtieth part of the "Richard and Benjamin" Pink** Edward Glover Master	05 : 00 : 00.
Item One Feather Bed and Steddle with the Appurtenances as it Stands	02 : 15 : 00.
Item Eleven pair of Sheets and one Odd Sheet of Course worn Linnen £2 . 17ˢ . 6ᵈ Four pillow Coates, one Table Cloth Two hand Towells 5ˢ. Three Chestes 6ˢ.	03 : 08 : 06.
Item Twelve old Mackrell netts	00 : 12 : 00.
Item Things unseen and forgotten	00 : 02 : 06.
The Totall Sume	13 : 08 : 00.

Taken the day and the year first above written
by us   Richard Legat
John Grover'

---

*Not until 1752 did Great Britain adopt the Gregorian Calendar which had been in use on the Continent since 1582. At the time of this document the New Year in Britain began on 25 March.
**One of the vessels mentioned in Defoe's *Storm*.

(A 'steddle' is what we now call a bedstead; 'course' is 'coarse';
pillow 'coates' are pillow cases).

Another widow, Mary Paine, although comparatively well off, being
worth over £93 (including £24 in cash and £54 in 'Sundry Debts due upon
Bills and for Rents & otherwise') must have been something of a miser for
her actual goods and chattels were fewer than Mrs Cobby's. Admittedly
she had some silver plate and rings worth £4, but otherwise, apart from
her clothes, all she owned was 'One Quilt, One Warming Pan and one
Frying pan, a Small Quantity of Wheate and Butter, Some Fire wood and
Seacoale [i.e. coal brought by sea], Lumber and things unseen and for-
gotten'. As there is no mention of bed, chairs, table and so on, she presumably rented furnished accommodation.

Both widows would appear to have lived in single rooms, probably as
lodgers in the kind of low-pitched dwelling which was described by
Brighton's earliest authenticated holiday-maker, the Rev. William
Clarke, rector of Buxted and a noted antiquary. Writing to a friend in
1736, he said 'I assure you that we live here almost underground. I fancy
that the architects here usually take the altitude of the inhabitants and
lose not an inch between the head and the ceiling, and then dropping a
step or two below the surface, the second storey is finished in something
under twelve feet. I suppose this was a necessary precaution against
storms, that a man should not be blown out of his bed into New England,
Barbary or God knows where. But as the lodgings are low they are cheap;
we have two parlours, two bed-chambers, pantry &c, for 5s per week; and
if you will really come down you need not fear a bed of the proper dimensions'.

Whatever their size they would have been built of local, readily available materials—either flints or 'the round sea-pebbles pitched in mortar'
to which young Joseph Jekyll (later an M.P. and Master in Chancery)
referred scornfully in 1775. Many examples of the use of such building
materials still survive in Brighton and elsewhere on the Sussex coast.

Most houses—like the Rev. Clarke's lodging—seem to have been of the
two-down-two-up variety (although often with a 'washhouse' or 'brewhouse' attached), but some were considerably more spacious. For
instance, there was a William Lane, who died in July, 1734. He was worth
only £84 apparently (£9 less than Widow Cobby) and yet his list of possessions indicate that he lived in considerable comfort and style. His
house had a Best Chamber, South Chamber, Back Chamber and North

Chamber (in other words, four first-floor bedrooms), a Hall, a Parlour, a kitchen, a pantry, a cellar, a stable and a brewhouse.

This last was quite a common feature of Brighton houses at this time, when the habit of drinking tea and coffee was only just beginning to filter down from the *beau monde* and beer was still the ordinary man's drink at every meal (as late as the early 1900's my mother, as a young girl, was given small beer at breakfast when she visited a New Forest farm). Thanks to Mr Lane's inventory we have a list of the equipment used for brewing: 'Two ffurnaces and Irons and Bricks—Fourteen Tubbs & Coolers—One Malt Ore 1 Tap Stick & Led 1 Brush'.

The 'coolers' were for cooling the wort or unfermented beer; the 'malt oar' was for stirring the mash; the 'tap stick' stopped the tap-hole of the mash tub; and the 'lead' was a leaden trough. In the cellar were the complimentary items: five barrels, a large funnel, three 'stolledges' (stands for casks) and two 'stoopers' (wedges) 'for to tilt ye Barrells'.

But change was taking place and is evidenced quite clearly by items in the inventories. For example, coal was replacing wood as fuel. From the reign of Elizabeth onwards the consumption of wood began to outrun supply, so that in some parts of the country there was an actual fuel famine. Those towns were fortunate that lay on the seaboard or a river, because—in the then state of the roads—they were virtually the only places remote from mining areas to which coal could be transported at a reasonable price. (It will be remembered that the vessel of which Tettersall was master was a coal-brig.) So, although most Brighton inventories of the early 1700's include 'brandirons', that is firedogs to support blazing logs, many of them also mention 'seacoal grates', which had been fitted into the existing hearths so that the new fuel could be used.

One resident who seems to have been something of a trend-setter was Henry Roberts. He is described as a mariner and was—the evidence suggests—a sea-captain. He died intestate in 1741, leaving to his widow, Hannah, goods and credits to the value of £367, most of this consisting of his two-thirds share in the brigantine *Unity*, which lay in Shoreham harbour. He was thus by no means the richest man in Brighton of this period (two yeomen had inventories of over £1,000 apiece) but the list of his possessions builds up a picture of a man who enjoyed living and had cultivated the art of doing it well.

For example, his was one of the few houses that had pictures on the walls and his table was able to show earthenware, stoneware and even china when most of his neighbours were still using pewter. He had his brewhouse and no less than four punch-bowls with over 40 drinking-glasses, but he also possessed a copper coffee-pot, five tea-pots, a glass sugar-dish and 'Fourteen China Teacups, 16 Ditto Saucers'.

He was not a reading man because, apart from a Bible and two Books of Common Prayer, his only other possession of this sort was '1 Book called the English Pylott' which he kept in a cupboard with his sea-chest, a quadrant and two 'Gunter's Scales' (a kind of slide-rule for navigational calculations). His telescope was in the parlour with two walking canes, so we can picture Henry Roberts spending his time ashore strolling the beach and casting a professional eye over the busy shipping lane until his silver watch told him it was noon and time for dinner.

There are also indications that Henry and Hannah had a full quiver. The cradle was tucked away in the attic, so presumably there were no babies in the family when he died, but the list of kitchen furniture tells us that not all the children were grown up. Two tables were not enough to accommodate the whole household at mealtimes because they had to be supplemented by a 'Sliding Board for a Table' and, in addition to seven ordinary chairs and a stool there were '3 more Chairs for Children'.

So it must have been a lively scene when they all sat down to a meal that had been cooked over a glowing coal-fire with the aid of '1 Jack 3 Spits 1 fire Shovell, 1 Poker and Tongs, 1 Frog [purpose unknown] 2 Trefts [trivets] 1 Sifter & Bellows', paraphernalia such as can still be seen—though on a suitably princely scale—in the Brobdingnagian kitchen of Brighton's Royal Pavilion.

In contrast to the Pickwickian flavour of the Roberts household, there are two inventories of a family called Deane that give an impression of frugal industry, of a rather feverish accumulation of money for its own sake rather than for any of the pleasures it could buy. Samuel Deane, a mariner like Roberts, was bachelor and lived with his widowed mother, Elizabeth; in a minimum of decent comfort but with none of the elegancies of the Roberts menage. His one-eight and one-quarter shares of fishing boats contributed only £14 to the £559 estate which he owned when he died in 1738. Its main constituents were £180 'due upon mortgages' and £320 'upon Several Bonds and Bills'.

The preamble to his will, which he made 13 years before he died, is worth giving for two reasons. Its lawyer-phrased religiosity is fairly standard for the period, while the final phrase shows a fatalistic appreciation of the dangers that faced a seaman:

'In the name of God I Samuel
Deane of Brighthelmstone in the County of Sussex Mariner being of a
Sound disposeing mind Memory and Understanding God be praised
Do by Divine permission make publish and declare these presents to be
and contain my last Will and Testament in manner following And first
I commend my Soul to God who gave it, and my Body I Committ to the
Earth or Sea as it shall please God to order . . . '

After his debts had been paid all his property went to his 'honoured
mother, Elizabeth Deane', who was also named as his executrix. She survived him for three years and did not squander her inheritance. Her estate
as shown in the inventory (and this, as we shall see, did not tell the whole
story) was worth nearly half as much again as her son's: £783, placing her
in the top four per cent—financially speaking—of Brighton's population.
She owned more upon mortgages (£258), but had less tied up on bond and
'upon Sundry Bills or notes of Hand'. However she seems to have started
pawnbroking in a small way as the sum of £18 was 'Due upon Plate and
Linnen taken upon a Pawn'. More important was the fact that, while
retaining her son's share in the two fishing boats, she had become sole
owner of 'One Snow or Vessell called the Samuel now lying in the River
Thames whereof Samuel Deane is Master'. (This Samuel Deane was a
nephew.) Here was a rise in the world for the Deane family, for a snow was
a two-masted square-rigger, a close relative of the brig and a cut above the
fishing boats, as its value of £250 indicated.

Her will was a much longer document than her son's, going into considerable finicking detail so that her wishes should not be misunderstood,
and it made clear that the inventory had not told the whole tale of the
Deane family's growing prosperity. She also owned three cottages: one in
East Street, one in North Street and one on the Steine (then an open space
where fishermen spread their nets to dry, but soon to become an area of
fashionable housing development). The first cottage went to some friends
or relatives called Jennings, the second to a kinswoman and the third to
her nephew, Samuel. In view of the later transformation of the town—
which so shrewd a woman may well have foreseen in 1741, when she made
her will—the Steine property was obviously the most valuable. Samuel
was a lucky fellow for, except for the other cottages and a few small
bequests, he inherited everything.

A surprisingly high proportion of the assets of a deceased person in
Brighton at this time consisted of debts due upon bonds and bills; some-

times these amounted to as much as 90 per cent of the total. A unique case was that of John Piercy, a prosperous mariner who had £100 'in the Stocks upon Government Security', in other words 'money in the Funds', like so many of the gentle spinster ladies in Jane Austen and Mrs Gaskell. This was a means of funding the National Debt which had been introduced in the reign of William and Mary and was intended to have particular appeal to the small investor who wanted a good safe interest to see out his lifetime; but in fact there were still only about 15,000 'fund-holders' at this date, so Piercy was somewhat ahead of his time (by 1829 there were more than 250,000).

But the townspeople's commonest form of investment was in ships or, more commonly, in the fishing fleet. Nearly every boat had several owners and nearly every investor had a share in two or more boats, usually a one-thirty-second share, but occasionally as little as a sixty-fourth. This made it less of a disaster to a single individual when a boat went down and made it easier to raise the money for a new one (part of the recorded assets of a widow who died in 1710 was £35 as 'Cash paid Towards Parte of a new Vessell now a Building').

Another popular way of spreading the load as an insurance against misfortune was to have more than one occupation. For instance, one of the richer men of the community, Israel Paine the shipwright, had, in addition to his main business of boat-building, shares in four pinks, a sloop and a ketch; and also ran a shop in which he sold nails, linen, tape, worsted, buttons, thread, laces, candles, pumice, starch, oatmeal, vinegar, pepper and spice; while the scale of his brewing equipment suggests a higher rate of production than would be needed for a single household. Most versatile of all, perhaps, was John Cox—described as a weaver, innkeeper and barber!

These manuscript sources do not confirm that picture of a lifeless waste that Defoe might have led us to expect. Times were undoubtedly hard but among the population there were clans tough and vigorous enough to keep what they had and perhaps gain a little more, to hold on grimly to their place in the social ladder and possibly to claw their way to the rung above. When John Burton—classical scholar and man-midwife —published a book of travels through Sussex in 1751 he summed up the people of Brighton as 'mostly very needy and wretched in their mode of living' but 'robust in their bodies, laborious, skilled in all nautical crafts, and, it is said, terrible cheats of the custom-house officers'.*

**Iter Sussexiense, translated by W. H. Blaauw (Sussex Archeological Collections, Vol. VIII)

None of them, thriving or hard-pressed, despairing or optimistic, could know that 1750 was to be the seed-year of a prosperity greater than Brighton had ever known before.

It was in that year that the Oxford University Press published a book called *De Tabe Glandulari: Sive Usu Aquae Marinae in Morbis Glandularum Dissertatio* (Glandular Diseases: or a Dissertation on the Use of Sea-Water in Affections of the Glands). It recommended immersion in and the drinking of sea-water as a remedy for a variety of bodily ills and particularly for 'the consumption which greatly afflicts our island, and in the cure of which our physicians find the greatest difficulty'.

Although the ideas expressed were not entirely new (both the ancient Greeks and English seamen of the day used sea-water as a purge) the book attracted immediate favourable notice among the medical profession: a pirated translation in 1752 and the author's own English version in the following year spread the message to a much wider audience and within a short time sea-bathing was something in which the entire world of fashion—and those who aspired to join its ranks—had to indulge.

Fortunately for Brighton, the author of this work, Dr Richard Russell, was in practice at Lewes. Presumably he sent his patients to Brighton for the cure because it was the nearest seaside place (nine miles away) which—with two inns and 400 houses—could provide the necessary amount of accommodation.

According to one writer,* the Rev. William Clarke, whose visit in 1736 we have already noticed, went to Brighton because Dr Russell recommended the sea-cure to his wife, so perhaps the preliminary stages of the town's re-birth had begun at least 14 years before the book.

The following recipe for a perfect bathing resort, which Dr Russell gave in a letter to a medical colleague, could well have been retrospective justification: ' . . . the situation of the place . . . should be clean and neat, at some distance from the opening of a river; that the water be as highly loaded with sea-salt and the other riches of the ocean as possible, and not weakened by the mixture of fresh water with its waves. In the next place one would choose the shore to be sandy and flat; for the convenience of going into the sea in a chariot. And lastly, that the seashore should be bounded by lively cliffs, and downs; to add to the cheerfulness of the place, and give the person that has bathed an opportunity of mounting on horseback dry and clean; to pursue such exercises, as may be advised by his

---

*J. D. Parry: *An Historical and Descriptive Account of the Coast of Sussex* (1833)

physician, when he comes out of the bath.'

Most of this fits Brighton with suspicious exactness, but the phrase 'sandy and flat' hardly applies to present-day Brighton's often steep banks of pebbles; perhaps the groynes of Dr Russell's day were less efficient in accumulating shingle than those built in later years. His 'chariots' were, of course, bathing machines, huts on wheels that horses would drag into such a depth of water that the bather could plunge without the tedium of a long wade. The timid would be accelerated by 'dippers', fishermen or their lusty wives who would grab and duck them.

Despite these rigorous procedures the number of visitors increased with phenomenal rapidity. Two prints, made 35 years apart give an immediately vivid impression of what was beginning to happen. The first, by C. Lemprière in 1743, shows a low huddle of cottages, less decrepit and more extensive than Defoe's wording would suggest, but still a humble place where people worked hard for small returns. Peter Mazell's drawing of the Steyne in 1778 shows it frequented by elegant strollers, with not a tarry fisherman in sight. A building standing by itself on the right is a circulating library. In the centre is the Castle inn, opened in 1755, with its assembly rooms that were added in 1766. (Its senior competitor, the Old Ship inn, kept up with the changing times by building a ballroom and cardroom in the following year.)* On the left of the picture is Marlborough House, built for the Duke of Marlborough nine years before, and the Manor House, also comparatively new.

It can be clearly seen in the picture that the Manor House is built of brick, a 'genteel' material so far as the older Brighton was concerned. Although many visitors would still be lodging in the cottages of pebble and flint that the Rev. Clarke described, speculators were quick to harvest the fruits of the town's new vogue. At the time of Lemprière's drawing there were 400–500 houses; when Mazell made his sketch there were at least 200 more than this.

A contemporary observer, writing in 1779, tells us exactly what kind of house was being built at that time (there are of course a great many of them still to be seen). He is Peregrine Phillips, the often caustic author of *A Diary kept in an Excursion to Littlehampton near Arundel and Brighthelmstone in Sussex*, usually referred to—from the name of its publisher—as *Bew's Diary*.

---

*These rooms at the 'Old Ship' are still the venue of the Regency Society banquets. The 'Castle' assembly rooms rebuilt on a new site in Montpelier Place are now St Stephen's Church for the deaf and dumb.

His entry for 7 September reads: 'Am viewing my worthy friend, Mr. Bull's house, or rather box, upon the Clift, between Ship Street and Black Lion Street. He beckons me in, and shews it throughout. It is one pretty room to the height of three stories, with a semi-circular window comprising most of the front, and on each overlooking the sea all ways, which makes the situation most delightful.' (This is a reference to the bow-windows which were to become and still remain one of the characteristic features of the town.)

Phillips also tells us how land values were soaring: 'The ground on which it stands is . . . nearly eighteen feet square . . . About fifty years ago this piece of land was sold for four pounds; thirty years since, a purchaser gave eleven; and about this time two years, the Alderman bought it for one hundred pounds to build upon.'

The fine frenzy of building which the maximum exploitation of well-to-do-visitors demanded still lay in the future, but already the town was of good enough report to attract immigrants. In 1760 there were only 2,000 inhabitants; their number had almost doubled by 1783—the year of an event that would make Brighton one of the fastest growing communities in Britain.

CHAPTER SIX

The Prince Regent

'Now a strange kind of bustle was heard through the town,
And what was the cause? . . . Why the Prince has come down,
In a phaeton drawn by six horses he came;
Where every steed had a sire of fame.
The men doft their hats and received him with claps,
The ladies all curtsey'd and cock'd up their caps.
The prince left his seat with the grace of God;
Then, smiling around him, return'd 'em a nod.'

G. S. Carey: *The Balnea* (1801)

The elevation of Brighton to such heights of distinction that, for over 40 years (at least so far as the world of fashion was concerned), it became virtually a second capital can be ascribed to two causes—one geographical and the other psychological.

The first is that it is only 50 miles from London. The second was the traditional propensity of members of the Royal family to be at odds with each other.

At a comparatively early stage of the town's career as a temple of health it began to be frequented by George III's brothers. The Duke of Gloucester stayed there in 1765, the Duke of York in 1766 and the Duke of Cumberland in 1771. The last of these became a regular visitor and rented the house on the Steine that had been built by Dr Russell (who had died in 1759).

In 1771 the Duke of Cumberland had married an Irish widow, Mrs Anne Horton, of whom the King disapproved so strongly that, in the following year, he caused a Royal Marriage Act to be passed which forbade any descendant of George II under 25 years of age to marry without the King's consent. This was one of two measures that were to create such problems of conscience for his eldest son and it is intriguing to recall a remark made during the Commons debate by that promising young politician, Charles James Fox. Opposing the Bill he prophesied that the

Prince of Wales (only nine years old at the time) would probably 'marry a woman without the consent of his father and live with her as his wife notwithstanding the act of parliament'.

The Royal Marriage Act initiated a feud between the King and Cumberland which was just as bitter ten years later, by which time the Prince was on equally bad terms with his father who, ever since his son's earliest boyhood had imposed on him a repressive regime ill-suited to so ebullient a temperament and bound to end in an explosion of defiance.

Since a shared hatred can be as strong a bond as a shared affection, uncle and nephew became cronies: an unfortunate conjunction since the older man was dissolute and the younger impatient to make a parade of independence. A correspondent of the *Morning Herald*, writing from Brighton in September 1782 described the Duke as the head of a 'motley group' given to 'every kind of amusement that fancy can desire for the train of folly and dissipation'.

It was in that year that Brighton's hopes of welcoming the heir to the throne first ran high, but it was not until the summer of 1783 that George, Prince of Wales, now 21 and so no longer running the risk of being humiliated by a paternal veto, announced his intention of joining the Duke.

He entered the town for the first time on 7 September, to be greeted with peals of bells from St Nicholas' Church and the booming of cannon from the battery on the sea-front. One of the charges exploded prematurely and killed a gunner, a sad shadow on the day in which the most felicitous of Brighton's historians, Osbert Sitwell, has discerned an appropriate symbolism: 'Brighton's great day had dawned, and as if to herald it, as if in imitation of more primitive days, when the tribe would assuredly have made some sacrifice to the God of Fortune, now arrived in the guise of the young Prince, the life of a man was offered up.'*

He was everything that a prince should be—tall, handsome, elegant, courteous; quick to smile, which pleased the ladies, and with a good seat on a horse, which was in those days a necessary article of acceptance by both sexes.

Every public detail of the visit was reported conscientiously by the *Sussex Weekly Advertiser*: 'At half after six the Heir Apparent and his royal uncle, the Duke of Cumberland, appeared on the Steine, where their Highnesses walked about half an hour, and then went to the rooms. Being Sunday evening the Steine was thronged with company, who flocked to

---

*Osbert Sitwell and Margaret Barton: *Brighton* (Faber and Faber, 1935)

see the royal guest. The town and Steine were illuminated, and the brilliancy of the evening concluded by a grand display of fireworks before the Duke of Cumberland's house'. Next day the royal gentlemen were out with the staghounds and in the evening attended a ball at the Castle inn.

Here it may be appropriate to sketch in the social routines, uncomplicated, even naïve perhaps by our standards, which were the framework of Brighton's 'high life' in 1783 and continued little changed for the next half-century.

An essential first step by the visitor on arrival was to enter his name and those of his wife and family in a register at one of the circulating libraries. By casting an eye over the preceding entries he was able to learn which of his friends and acquaintances were already in the town and consider how best he might meet (or avoid) them. If he had daughters of marriageable age he could identify the field of suitable bachelors; if he was himself a bachelor and of the needy sort, he could short-list the available young ladies of fortune.

As we saw in the preceding chapter, there were by now two taverns, the Old Ship and the Castle, each wishing to arrange social occasions for the entertainment of the nobility and gentry and for the more numerous bourgeoisie who, although neither noble or gentle, were happy to pay for the privilege of rubbing shoulders with those who were.

Somewhat surprisingly the proprietors of these two establishments were quick to perceive that they had more to gain from a concordat than by competition. Mutually satisfactory arrangements were made possible by the introduction of a professional functionary of a kind whose usefulness had already been demonstrated at the inland spa of Bath: the Master of Ceremonies. Thanks to his arbitration it was agreed that there should be a ball every Monday at the Castle and every Thursday at the Ship; 'card assemblies' were held four times a week, twice at each establishment; and on alternate Sunday evenings the Castle or the Ship would hold a 'Promenade and Public Tea'.

The Master of Ceremonies was also the essential link between the visitors' book and the social programme. He would call upon new arrivals and provide them with invitations to the various assemblies; and, if an impecunious lieutenant of Foot confided his interest in the wealthy Miss X, could at least ensure that their paths would cross from time to time.

There were of course many other innocent entertainments: the theatre, cricket matches, horse-racing, dinner parties, endless gossip on the Steyne and in the libraries. But Brighton soon acquired the reputation for raffishness and illicit pleasures which has in varying degrees been part of its aura (and often one of its cardinal attractions) ever since. The *Morning Post* of 4 August 1785 referred to its invasion by a female *corps d'amour* and added primly: 'Women of virtue and character shun these scenes of debauchery and drunkenness ever attendant on the spot which is the temporary residence of a ....'

No reader failed to supply the missing word or was in any doubt as to which prince was meant. A sentence in Robert Huish's *Memoirs of George the Fourth* (1831) gives us the picture of the Prince of Wales which already existed in the public mind and would persist: 'With every fresh amour his appetite appeared to be sharpened—like the bee he roamed from flower to flower, sipped the honey, but never visited that flower again.'

Oddly enough this was one of the periods in the Prince's life when such a stricture was unjustified, for it was in that year after a single-minded courtship often bordering on frenzy that he married a virtuous Catholic lady, six years older than himself and already twice widowed: Mrs Maria Fitzherbert (the three wedding rings can be seen—picked out in gold leaf—on the portrait statue near her tomb in the Church of St John the Baptist at Bristol Road, Brighton).

By contemporary account she was beautiful, although some of her own sex criticised her nose as too aquiline, her chin as too strong and her bosom as overflowing. All agreed that her golden hair and clear complexion were her own. If she did incline to plumpness she had two qualities that often go with it and men have always found commendable: serenity as she listened and animation when she spoke. Even in old age, said Lady Hester Stanhope, she remained 'physically delicious'.

No one has been able to formulate a completely satisfactory explanation of the emotional dovetail that linked these two people together to the end of their lives despite physical separation and wanton acts of mental cruelty by the Prince. Maria's appeal to him is understandable. Her motherly nature helped to abolish the hangovers of a joyless childhood and provided intervals of tranquillity in a life which would otherwise have had no direction but *fortissimo*.

But why should the Prince have appealed to her? In an age when any new liaison in the upper reaches of society became journalistic property within hours no scandal ever attached to her name and her long avoidance of the Prince's advances would hardly suggest that she was driven into his arms by sexual appetite. Nor was it ever hinted that she shared his bed with political motives, even though many women of her time and station played Whig-and-Tory shuttlecock as enthusiastically as men; while her subsequent conduct patently absolved her of any designs on the throne. Finally, she can hardly have been in any doubt as to the Prince's philandering and his penchant for rackety companions like Sir John Lade, stunted in body and mind, whose wife was a former mistress of Sixteen-String-Jack the highwayman.

On the credit side it might be said that the Prince's circle also included Charles James Fox, the eloquent Whig, and Sheridan, the playwright, who—although not models of decorum—at least had brains and wit; that he had an excellent taste in music and painting; that he could be a charming host (when he resisted the temptation to play practical jokes); and could show genuine kindness to humble people in misfortune. Perhaps it was this softer side that won Mrs Fitzherbert's heart; perhaps one has to be content with the oldest and least enlightening of answers, that she loved him.

The first words she heard him speak were flattering if unceremonious. Still wearing widow's weeds, she was leaving the Opera, escorted by her uncle, Henry Errington, when the Prince accosted them: 'Who the devil is that pretty girl you have on your arm, Henry?'

From that moment he made no secret of his feelings. He would attend no ball or banquet unless assured she would be there; he called daily at her London house. She gave him no encouragement, making it clear that in no circumstances would she become his mistress and assuming marriage to be out of the question. The main obstacle of course was her Roman Catholic faith. Feeling against her co-religionists was so strong that in William III's reign the Act of Settlement had been passed to exclude any Catholic from succeeding to the Throne (it was not until 1827 that they were even allowed to sit in Parliament). Obviously George III would never agree to the heir marrying a Catholic and, as we have seen, the Prince was forbidden by the Royal Marriage Act to marry without his father's consent before he was 25.

Faced with her quiet refusals the Prince swore he would give up all rights to the throne and, if even then she would not accept him, he would commit suicide. On 8 July 1784, he did in fact stab himself in the chest with a sword and, when Mrs Fitzherbert was summoned to his bedside, extorted from her some sort of promise that she would marry him. Justifiably she did not consider herself bound by a promise so obtained, fled to France and spent the next 18 months travelling round Europe.

Meanwhile the Prince, unable to leave England without his father's permission, continued his protestations of devotion in a mounting wave of hysteria. According to Lord Holland he 'cried by the hour' and 'testified to the sincerity and violence of his passion and his despair by the most extravagant expression and actions, rolling on the floor, striking his forehead, tearing his hair, falling into hysterics, and swearing he would abandon the country, forfeit the crown, sell his jewels and plate, and scrape together a competence to fly with the object of his affections to America'.

To the 'best and most sacred of women' in her various Continental retreats he directed a stream of letters (one of them 42 pages long), assuring her of 'his wishes to be the best of husbands' and signing himself 'Unalterably Thine'.

Eventually she gave in. She returned to England and on 15 December 1785, they were married secretly. The ceremony was performed at her London house in Park Street by Mr Burt, an Anglican clergyman, whom the Prince had delivered from the Fleet Prison by paying off the £500 debt for which he was held. The witnesses were Maria's brother, Jack Smythe, and her uncle, that same Henry Errington who had first introduced her to the Prince. Although it was a Church of England ceremony the Roman Catholic Church regarded it as valid.

Thus began the first period of their life together, when they divided their time equally between Brighton and London, maintained separate households at both places, but were received as man and wife in the best society (except at Court).

It was in October 1789 that they received some unusual visitors at the Prince's Brighton residence—not the Oriental Palace which is now the town's chief tourist attraction, but an earlier building on the same site: a Palladian villa with bow windows and a central domed rotunda. Their guests were from France, first heralds of a strife that was to engulf Europe for the next quarter of a century. They were the Marquis and the Marquise d'Osmond, with their eight-year-old daughter, Adèle, who had all been with the French Court at Versailles when the Palace was raided by the revolutionary mob that carried off the King and Queen to the Tuileries.

Little Adèle was to grow up to be the Comtesse de Boigne, whose four-volume memoirs provide a highly personalised but eminently readable view of French affairs (as seen from the top) from this period until the 1860's. The Marquise (a Miss Dillon before her marriage) was cousin to Mrs Fitzherbert, who had stayed with her in Paris during her flight from the Prince.

'We landed at Brighton', says the Comtesse in her memoirs, 'and whom should my mother encounter—at the very moment of landing—but Mrs Fitzherbert, who happened to be strolling on the quay! . . . I well remember being taken by Mrs Fitzherbert one morning to the Prince's dressing room, where there was a huge table completely covered with shoe-buckles! I gave a cry of delight when I saw them, upon which Mrs Fitzherbert smiling, flung open a cabinet which was filled with as many more. The prince had one for every day of the year! This was the age of dandies and he was their *nonpareil*. So magnificent a collection made such an impression on my childish imagination that for many years afterwards the Prince of Wales figured in my mind only as the owner of all those shoe-buckles.'

More and more emigrés were to land on Brighton beach as the reign of terror intensified and in 1793 the war with France broke out that was to continue, almost without a break, for more than 20 years. The old fear of invasion returned and great tented camps of regular troops and militia sprung up on the Downs behind the town. But in the assembly rooms the French threat was soon a less favoured topic than the rumour that the Prince and Mrs Fitzherbert were to separate.

The trouble, as so often in his life, was his frantic and incurable extravagance. He was in debt to the tune of £375,000 and his father would only wipe the slate clean if he would ensure the Protestant succession by marrying a German princess. Of those available the Prince—unwisely and to his lasting regret—chose jolly, clumsy, dottily tactless Caroline of Brunswick.

With the sadistic abruptness which was his invariable recourse when his conscience irked him, he abandoned Mrs Fitzherbert in 1794 as if there had been no marriage ceremony, no nine years of chequered domesticity. The sole mitigation of his offence was that he continued her allowance of £3,000 a year.

Yet on 7 April 1795, the night before his marriage, this strangely jumbled man said to his brother, the Duke of Clarence: 'William, tell Mrs Fitzherbert she is the only woman I shall ever love'. And in the following January when he had a fever and thought he was going to die, he made a will leaving all his property to 'my Maria Fitzherbert, my wife, the wife of my heart and soul . . .'.

One of the side-effects of the French war—as prints of the period show—is that elegant dragoons began to appear among the strollers on the Steyne, causing a flutter in female hearts that Jane Austen describes in

Pride and Prejudice: 'In Lydia's imagination a visit to Brighton comprised every possibility of earthly happiness. She saw, with the creative eye of fancy, the streets of that gay bathing place covered with officers. She saw herself the object of attention to tens and scores of them at present unknown. She saw all the glories of the camp—its tents stretched forth in beauteous uniformity of lines, crowded with the young and gay, and dazzling with scarlet; and, to complete the view, she saw herself beneath a tent, tenderly flirting with at least six officers at once.'

But flirtations and elegance were not the sum of eighteenth-century life; pain and cruelty were never far away. It was a world in which soldiers and sailors were disciplined with the cat-o'-nine-tails, surgeons operated without anaesthetics, Latin grammar was flogged into the sons of the rich and a son of the poor could go to the gallows for stealing a handkerchief.

A public spectacle of particular horror took place on 13 June 1795 in a downland valley at Goldstone Bottom, Hove, following a court-martial in Brighton.

Troops encamped in the area had been complaining and agitating about the quality of the bread and flour supplied with their rations. To demonstrate the strength of their discontent some of the men of the Oxford Militia broke into a mill and later emptied a ship's cargo of corn into the Ouse. Eight men were tried for mutiny. Two were sentenced to death by a firing party of their own regiment and the rest were to receive 300 lashes each. The sentences were duly carried out (except that three of the men were let off their flogging) in the full view of 13 regiments of infantry. It must have been a very tense, touch-and-go situation with the officers fearful that even the iron bonds of eighteenth-century discipline would not restrain the assembled troops from a seething mêlée of indignation, for J. A. Erredge in his *History of Brighthelmstone* (1862) speaks of 'the Artillery being planted on the right, with lighted matches, in the rear of the Oxfordshire, to prevent any mutiny, if attempted, and the whole height commanded by two thousand cavalry'.

Erredge tells us that, after the troops had marched away, the shepherd 'whose innocent flocks browsed where so tragic an affair had occurred' cut out slabs of turf to mark the shape of coffins and the position of the firing squad, which he pointed out to interested visitors for many years afterwards. There is small doubt that, in so doing, the shepherd had 'an eye to business', for which the local inhabitants—anxious to make up for all those lean years—were now acquiring a certain notoriety.

For instance, the following stanzas appeared in a London newspaper in

1796, attributed to 'a Gentleman leaving Brighthelmstone, on his observing a gilt Shark placed as a Weathercock on top of the Church' (in strict accuracy it was a dolphin):

> *Say, why on Brighton's Church we see*
> *A golden shark display'd,*
> *But that't was aptly meant to be*
> *An emblem of its trade?*
> *Nor could the thing so well be told*
> *In any other way;*
> *The town's a shark that lives on gold,*
> *The Company its prey.*

Some of 'the Company' deserved no better of Brighton if we are to believe 'Anthony Pasquin'. This was the pen-name of a Welshman, John Williams, reputed to have drawn much of his income in hush-money paid by people he promised *not* to write about.

His *Twelve Golden Rules for Young Gentlemen of Distinction, to be Observed at Brighton for the Year 1796* may be satire but one suspects the truth needed little touching-up:

'Young and inexperienced officers must confederate with several of their mess as young as themselves, and reel into the theatre during the performance in a state of assumed intoxication, and be sure to disturb the audience in the most interesting part of the drama, by taking liberties with any of those Cyprian nymphs [i.e. prostitutes] who harbour in the green boxes . . . '

There were complementary rules for young ladies who were advised

' . . . to be the first in getting into a carriage, if there be men in the company, that they may have a complete occasion of showing a well-turned ancle; or if they should be proportioned like the Medicean Venus, they should affect a hoyden air, and in jumping into the phaeton or curricle, contrive to stumble upon their knee, as by that method it is an hundred to one, but the whole of one, or both limbs, is exposed to the searching eyes of the accompanying beaus, who will not fail to communicate to all they know, as a great secret, that Miss Such-a-one has a d---d handsome leg'.

These beauties and their beaux might tolerate the aboriginal population as picturesque background decoration but they did not relish them at close quarters. G. S. Carey (in *The Balnea*, 1799) complained that 'fishing nets are daily spread from one end of the Stayné to the other, so that the company, while walking, are frequently tripped up by entangling their feet; and if any one of the barbarians to whom the nets belonged should be standing by, you are sure to be reprobated and insulted for what you cannot avoid.'

The drying of the nets on the Steine, wrote a Welsh zoologist, Thomas Pennant, was 'a privilege time immemorial, granted to the fishermen' (there were to be resentful demonstrations in 1822 when the Steine was railed off and the privilege withdrawn).

Their life was as hard as it had always been and it is little wonder that they looked on these idlers with a less than kindly eye. 'They set sail generally in the evening', Pennant noted, 'go eight or ten leagues to sea, and return the next day. The fishing is always carried on at night . . . during the summer season, they have very small interval from labour. They get a good meal, and a very short repose by lying themselves on a bed during the few hours in the day on which they come ashore.'

In addition to the normal hazards of the sea they now had to face—as so many of their ancestors had done—the possibility of capture by the French. A typical incident is described by James Charles Michell, editor of the 1829 edition of Brighton's first guide-book, *A Short History of Brighthelmston*, which Dr Anthony Relhan (Russell's successor) had written in 1761: 'In November, 1798, it pleased the Jacobin Government of France to extend its crimes by waging war with the unoffending and unarmed fishermen of this town, 27 of whom were taken prisoners, and conveyed under the usual circumstances of barbarity then so prevalent in that nation into the interior of the country. The poor fellows were exchanged after three months' detention, and returned in rags and exhaustion to their families.'

But such plebeian matters were a less than nine days' wonder when Brighton began to susurrate with rumours of a reconciliation at the Pavilion.

For five years the Prince of Wales and 'the wife of his heart and soul' had never met—except as strangers in public places. But by 1799 the lack of Maria's comforting presence (and perhaps some overdue stirrings of remorse?) were affecting the Prince to such a degree that there was a noticeable deterioration in his health. Several members of the Royal family—including the Queen, his mother—begged her to be reconciled. In an agony of self-examination, still loving him, but flinching from the possibility of fresh indignities, she asked Rome for guidance. The Papal answer was that she must regard herself as 'the only true wife' of the Prince. So, in 1800, they were re-united and again became part of the Brighton scene.*

For glimpses of their life in the Pavilion we can turn to Thomas Creevey, the Whig politician whose memoirs are a rich source for the gossip and atmosphere of the period. He arrived in Brighton in September, 1805, accompanied by his wife (her letters complement the memoirs), who now met Mrs Fitzherbert for the first time and became her lifelong friend.

If we had not already met the phenomenon in the pages of Jane Austen we of the 'total war' century might be astonished by the extent to which the civilians of this island could be literally 'insulated' from the fighting. In 1805, as Napoleon was leading 200,000 men against Austria and Prussia and Nelson was trying to draw the combined French and Spanish fleets out of Cadiz harbour for the battle we know as Trafalgar, Creevey was able to record as follows:

'We used to dine pretty punctually at six, the average number being sixteen . . . Mrs Fitzherbert was a great card-player, and played every night. The Prince never touched a card, but was occupied in talking to his guests, and very much in listening to and giving directions to the band. At twelve o'clock punctually the band stopped, and sandwiches and wine and water handed about, and shortly after the Prince made a bow and we all dispersed. I had heard a great deal of the Prince's drinking, but, during the time that I speak of, I never saw him the least drunk but once . . . He used to drink a great quantity of wine at dinner, and was very fond of making any newcomer drunk by drinking wine with him frequently, always recommending his strongest wines, and at last some remarkable strong old brandy which he called Diabolino.'

Far from concealing the nameless orgies which many have delighted or shuddered to imagine, the Pavilion seems to have had the skylarking atmosphere of a boys' preparatory school at the end of term, as instanced

*From 1804 onwards Mrs Fitzherbert's establishment was Steine House—on the Steine (now occupied by the Y.M.C.A.).

by the roguishness of Sheridan during a 'phantasmagoria'—a series of optical illusions of a 'ghostly' sort produced by a magic lantern, which were a fashionable novelty in 1805. 'Sheridan', writes Creevey, 'entered into whatever fun was going on at the Pavilion as if he had been a boy, tho' he was then 55 years of age. Upon one occasion he came into the drawing-room disguised as a police officer to take up the Dowager Lady Sefton for playing at some unlawful game; and at another time, when we had a phantasmagoria at the Pavilion, and were all shut up in perfect darkness, he continued to sit upon the lap of Madame Gerobtzoff, a haughty Russian dame, who made row enough for the whole town to hear her.'

Or there is this excerpt from a letter dated 29 October 1805, that Creevey received from his wife: ' . . . the Prince led all the party to the table where the maps lie, to see him shoot with an air-gun at a target placed at the end of the room. He did it very skilfully and wanted all the ladies to attempt it. The girls and I excused ourselves on account of short sight; but Lady Downshire hit a fiddler in the dining room, Miss Johnstone a door and Bloomfield the ceiling . . . '.

The host at these eccentric parties was, of course, no longer the Prince Charming of 1783. Caricatures of this later date emphasise his paunch and jowls but we have a less prejudiced picture of him, as seen through the eyes of a small boy in 1806 and recollected by him when, as Lord Albemarle, he wrote *Fifty Years of My Life* in 1876: 'A merry, good-humoured man, tall, though somewhat portly in stature, in the prime of life, with laughing eyes, pouting lips and nose which, very slightly turned up, gave a peculiar poignancy to the expression of his face.'

After reading this description it is not surprising to learn that, in her old age, Maria looked back on this period as one in which he and she were 'as merry as crickets'. But her happiness was not to last and seems to have been undermined long before she suspected anything was amiss.

George III had first suffered from mental illness in 1788 and as, after the turn of the century, his madness became more and more marked, the Prince began to fear that his continuing association with a 'Papist' might prove an obstacle to his becoming Regent, a position which he coveted as a final signal of freedom. His manner towards Mrs Fitzherbert became noticeably cooler and in 1811, a few months after he assumed the Regency, he broke with her completely.

His new inamorata—impeccably Protestant—was the Marchioness of Hertford, who had been establishing her hold over him for some years. As far back as 1807 that sharp-eyed Irish beauty the Hon. Mrs Calvert had noted in her diary: 'Last night we went to a ball at Lady Hertford's. I think poor Mrs Fitzherbert much deserted by him now. He has taken it into his head to fall desperately in love with Lady Hertford . . . without exception the most forbidding, haughty, unpleasant-looking woman I ever saw.'

Every contemporary account of the Prince tends to increase one's confusion regarding his personality. As a young man he had overflowed with energy of the most dynamic kind (in 1784 he had ridden horseback from Brighton to London and back again in ten hours), but it had always been denied any useful outlet. For example, he was deeply mortified that his father would never let him go on active service in the long and bitter war that might have ended in Britain's reduction to satellite status in a French Empire. There was no suggestion that he was any less brave than his brothers who smelt gunpowder but—as heir to the throne—he was denied any military duty more warlike than reviewing troops on the Downs.

He had—or gossip of the day chose to credit him with—a long string of mistresses; he took nine-course meals that could last four or five hours; he drank heavily. None of this was unusual for a man of his period and station, but in his case these indulgences had a frenetic quality that seemed the symptom of a deep unhappiness.

Had he not been a king's son he would probably have made a good soldier, a contented husband and a fond father. As it was, only his first sojourn with Mrs Fitzherbert seems to have given him any peace of mind and once he decided that his birthright must take precedence over domesticity he resorted to a form of escapism to which the rich and idle have always been particularly prone. At the end of his life his fantasies would break out into words and he would relate with great circumstantiality his exploits at the battle of Waterloo, but much earlier they had found expression in bricks and mortar.

In 1808 the new Royal Stables and Riding House was completed in the Pavilion grounds. Costing over £54,000 and taking five years to construct, it dwarfed every other building in its vicinity. Its most striking feature was the circular cupola of wood and glass, 80 feet in diameter covering a central circular court, round which were two tiers of Moorish arches—the lower ones leading to 44 stalls for the horses and the upper to ostlers' quarters and harness rooms (the scale can be judged from the fact that it is now used as a concert- and conference-hall housing audiences of 2,000).

Oriental designs were holding an increasing fascination for the Prince.

Already the interior of the Pavilion had been decorated and furnished with *chinoiserie* and in 1803 drawings were prepared which, if accepted, would have given the exterior the likeness of a Chinese pagoda.

However, the mosque-like appearance of his new stables had turned the Prince's mind in the direction of India and in 1815 the versatile John Nash, architect of London's Regent Street, began the project which would extend and improve the interior of the building and give it the outward aspect it now bears—that of a *bijou* Taj Mahal. He it was who introduced some of the features which modern visitors find amusingly quaint but were, in their day, an indication of that mastery of new technology that was giving Britain a world lead in the first Industrial Revolution: delicate 'bamboo' balustrades to the staircases—made of cast iron; theatrical 'palm trees' supporting the roof of the immense kitchen, their leaves of copper and their trunks . . . cast iron.

So the end result was an Indian building with Chinese décor, the whole having a Hollywoodish charm that is a pleasure to the eye in an age of high-rise egg-boxes, but horrified most contemporaries and was not to be accepted by the *cognoscenti* until Sir Osbert Sitwell commended it in his book on Brighton in 1935.

A French lady stayed there in 1818, when it was nearly in its final form, although the finishing touches would not be made until 1821. She was the same Adèle who had admired the Prince's shoe-buckles in 1789, but now 37 years old and Comtesse de Boigne.

'The Pavilion was a masterpiece of bad taste', she wrote in her memoirs. 'Here at immense expense one had brought together from the four corners of the globe a collection of curiosities—of the most sumptuous kind, admittedly—and heaped them all together under the eight (or is it ten?) cupolas of this bizarre, ugly palace, this hotch-potch of styles completely lacking in unity and surely not worthy of the name of architecture. The arrangement of the interior was no better and certainly had nothing to do with art.'

Then some kinder words: 'But there my criticism ends. In no other establishment was there better understanding of the arts of comfort and pleasure; and, having—as a salaam to the gods of good taste—disparaged this fantastic amalgam of curiosities, one could enjoy oneself endlessly in examining all the fine detail of this costly extravaganza.'

Kindest of all were her comments on the Pavilion's owner: 'One could not have a more attentive host than the Regent. If he wished to please you, he would overwhelm you with kindness, making it a personal task to look

1 A 16th-century representation of Brighton being burned down by French sea-raiders. It bears the date of July 1545 but almost certainly refers to an event which took place 31 years earlier.

2　The oldest dwelling in Brighton. A 15th-century timber-framed cottage, it is in the Moulsecoomb district at the rear of an early 19th-century house, Moulsecoomb Place.

3　The 18th-century facade of Patcham Place conceals the thick Tudor walls of flint and rubble. In the first half of the 17th century it was the home of Anthony Stapley, one of the signatories of Charles I's death-warrant. It is now used as a youth hostel.

4   Brighton as it looked in 1743, when it still relied for the most part on its sailors and fishermen for a livelihood and had not yet come into fashion as a sea-water spa. From a drawing by C. Lemprière.

5   The Steine at Brighton in 1778, when new buildings were springing up to meet the needs of fashionable visitors. The third building from the left is Marlborough House, built for the fourth Duke of Marlborough. In 1786 Robert Adam designed a new building on the same site, which is now the town's information office for tourists. From a drawing by Peter Mazell.

6   Dr Richard Russell, of Lewes, whose treatise on the virtues of sea-bathing initiated Brighton's popularity with the world of fashion, built this house at the seaward end of the Steine in 1753. At the time that this drawing was made by the Hon. James Luttrell (in 1786) it was the residence of the Duke of Cumberland, uncle to the Prince of Wales. The Royal Albion Hotel now stands on the site.

OUT OF FITS,
or THE RECOVERY TO THE SATISFACTION OF ALL PARTIES.

Published 6th May 1786, by S. W. Fores, at the Caricature Warehouse, No. 3, Piccadilly.

7 and 8   The clandestine marriage of the Prince of Wales to twice-widowed Maria Fitzherbert — in December 1785 — did not remain a secret for long. These evidences of public interest in the event were published at 'The Caricature Warehouse, No. 3, Piccadilly' in May and September of the following year.

TAFFY AND HUR WIFE, SHENTLEMAN OF WALES.

9   Brighton beach in about 1795; a water-colour by Richard Earlom. The wheeled cabins which were drawn into the sea for the greater convenience of bathers can be seen in the centre of the picture.

10   The Pavilion and the Steine in 1806; from an aquatint by Cracklow. The open space where fishermen used to dry their nets has become a promenade for those anxious to see or be seen by the Prince of Wales. He himself, on horseback, is at the right of the picture. The domed Pavilion is still in Italianate style, prior to its Oriental transformation.

11 Between 1815 and 1821 John Nash gave the Pavilion its Indian exterior. This contemporary engraving by J. Cordwell, of East Street, Brighton, is particularly interesting because it includes a rare illustration of a 'Brighton Fly' — a sedan-chair on wheels — designed for his own use in 1809 by a local tradesman who had been crippled in an accident. Copies of this vehicle were so popular with the Prince and his cronies for midnight excursions that they came to be known as 'fly-by-nights'. Later versions were horse-drawn.

12 and 13   Two of John Nash's *Views of the Royal Pavilion*, Published in 1826 from drawings by A. C. Pugin. The Chinese décor of the interior can be seen in the corridor (above) — as it appeared in 1815; and in the magnificent music-room (below), which was severely damaged by fire in 1975. Restoration, costing about £250,000, will take several years.

14   In the 1820's and 1830's a new and elegant residential quarter was built in open country to the east of Brighton by Thomas Read Kemp and it still bears his name — Kemp Town. Lewes Crescent — here shown in G. B. Campion's water-colour of 1838 — has a diameter 200 feet greater than that of the Royal Crescent at Bath.

15   An impression by *Punch* artist C. J. Grant of the London-to-Brighton stage-coach in early Victorian times. Until well into the 18th century Sussex roads were notoriously bad, but by 1828 a French visitor was able to report that the journey took only seven hours, over 'a road as smooth and well-gravelled as a garden path'.

THE 3 BROWNS BOOK'D FOR BRIGHTON, AND ONLY ONE PLACE.

16 'Brighton, England's Favourite Watering Place', an aquatint of 1825, by Sutherland, shows the Chain Pier, completed two years before. It was to suffer much damage by storms and was finally destroyed in 1896.

17 One of the few pictures of Queen Victoria against a Brighton background. By an unknown artist, it was published as a coloured lithograph in 1838 and entitled: 'Her Most Gracious Majesty, Victoria 1st, as she appeared at the Royal Pavilion, Brighton, previous to her mounting her favourite Arabian horse'.

18 and 19 Two stages in the development of Brighton as a seaside resort. J. Morse's drawing 'Morning Promenade on the Cliff, Brighton, 1806', is obviously concerned with comparatively small numbers of people, even though it depicts cheerful bustle of the kind Betsey Trotwood so abhorred. In contrast, the water-colour, 'Brighton Beach, 1864', by 'Cuthbert Bede' (Edward Bradley), offers striking evidence of the mass invasion which followed the opening of the London–Brighton railway line in 1841 and the introduction of cheap-day excursion trains three years later.

20 and 21 The Brighton and Rottingdean Seashore Railway, popularly known as 'The Daddy-Long-Legs', was opened in 1896 by Magnus Volk, Brighton-born son of an immigrant German clockmaker. The track ran underwater and the double-decker 150-passenger car was mounted on iron stilts, 24 feet high. Angela Thirkell, the novelist, who saw it at Rottingdean as a child, said it was 'more like a vision of the Martians than anything you ought to see in a peaceful seaside village'. It existed for only four years.

22 and 23 Mechanisation comes to Rottingdean. Frederick Thomas, landlord of the 'Royal Oak', ran a horse-bus service between Rottingdean and Brighton railway station in the 1890's. In the first photograph he can be seen, wearing a straw boater, on the top deck of a three-horse vehicle driven by his son, George. In the second picture, taken about 1900, he is standing by the bonnet of his newly-acquired motor-bus and the boater has been exchanged for a chauffeur's cap.

24   Brighton's West Pier, opened in 1866 'as a means of recreation and health', is here shown in its heyday (around 1900) when attendances on a Sunday would exceed 10,000. It is now in a state of dilapidation and threatened with demolition, but local residents have mounted a determined and highly vocal 'We Want the West Pier' campaign to find ways of saving it.

25 Brighton front (near the bottom of West Street) at about the time King Edward VII came to the throne. The hawker with his back to the camera has a shellfish stall and the woman — probably an Italian at that period — is selling hokey-pokey, hard-frozen ice-cream. Note the bowler-hatted man on the right with a Long John Silver wooden leg.

26 During the General Strike in 1926 there was a clash between strikers and police which a local newspaper headlined as 'The Battle of Lewes Road'. The photograph shows a body of mounted special constables — which figured prominently in the incident — mustering in front of the Town Hall.

to the veriest minutiae of your comfort. For instance, you had only to dine at his table two or three times and he would familiarise himself with the dishes you liked and go to great trouble to see they were placed before you. Such attentions are particularly flattering when they come from someone of high degree (and those who make the greatest show of their indifference to rank are the ones who enjoy them most!). I never knew anyone whom the Prince could not captivate with his charm when he wanted to.'

And yet, in 1827, George IV—as he had by then become—abandoned the palace which he had built as a refuge from the bothersome world and never again returned to the town which had beguiled him for over 40 years.

The Duke of Wellington tells us of the reason—or rather he tells us *part* of the reason, for he withholds one essential item of information with a characteristically Olympian disregard for so human an emotion as curiosity.

Earl Stanhope in his published *Notes of Conversations with the Duke of Wellington* gives the following entry for 8 October 1839, when he breakfasted with the great man at Walmer Castle: ' . . . the conversation turned upon writing on windows with a diamond pencil. The Duke said that as great things spring from little ones, it was some scribbling of this kind that prevented George the Fourth from ever returning to Brighton. For a lady at the Pavilion (it is not difficult to guess who), having her attention called—probably by her maid or some such person—to some words on a window written with a diamond and reflecting severely upon herself, declared in her passion she would never return to the place—nor did she, nor the King either. And this was the secret but undoubted reason for his keeping away from Brighton ever since.'

We know the identity of the lady; she was Lady Conyngham, Lady Hertford's successor in the Royal favour. But no one yet knows what the words were that so offended her.

The Duke is one of two people to blame for a far greater and more irritating mystery. In the cause of discretion (which he considered a paramount virtue) he committed what historians can only regard as a gross act of vandalism. It centres round Maria Fitzherbert.

Living with her at Brighton were two young ladies always referred to as her 'adopted daughters'. One of these was Mary (generally known as 'Minney') Seymour who was—ostensibly—the orphan daughter of Lord and Lady Seymour, although the Prince apparently believed himself to be the father. The other was Marianne Smythe, thought by some to be the illegitimate daughter of Mrs Fitzherbert's brother, Jack; by others to be Maria's own child by the Prince.

Some intriguing speculations on the subject are to be found in Anita Leslie's *Mrs Fitzherbert*,* the most perceptive and satisfying of the books about Maria, almost certainly because Miss Leslie is Minney's great-great-granddaughter. 'Although there could not have been any real danger of a Catholic pretender to England', she writes, 'the topic of possible children remained a dangerous one even after Mrs Fitzherbert's death. Minney Seymour preserved the miniatures of two children *sans nom* who, she whispered, were Mrs Fitzherbert's. A boy and a girl whose fate cannot definitely be proved . . . It seems very possible that Marianne Smythe, the quietly adopted niece of Mrs Fitzherbert, was her own daughter, but this girl could have been Jack Smythe's illegitimate daughter (his wife was barren). As for the nebulous son—a yet more dangerous element—what happened to him? Poor little fellow, he must have been hustled out of the way when very tiny. There are few clues—just a miniature and a few whispers echoing in two English families, while the Jesuits at Georgetown in America keep a picture and a legend.'

Some of the correspondence which passed between the Prince and his first bride still exists at Windsor Castle and elsewhere, but much that could have satisfied the curiosity of posterity was destroyed. After George IV died Mrs Fitzherbert returned all his letters to his executor, the Duke of Wellington, who promptly burned them. She received all her own letters in exchange.

Miss Leslie goes on to describe the equally horrifying destruction of evidence by Minney's daughter and her own great-grandmother, Lady Constance Leslie: 'My great-grandmother was, alas, a true Victorian; she ransacked her husband's letter-chests, censoring and mutilating with nail-scissors improper eighteenth-century Leslie correspondence concerning their eternal bastards, and then, far worse, she got busy on the Fitzherbert papers. Although she carefully docketed and annotated her mother's records of what was an illegal but undoubtedly virtuous alliance she destroyed all reference to Mrs Fitzherbert's issue. Lady Constance possessed, apart from her mother's papers, a mysteriously locked box inscribed "Duke of Cornwall" (the Prince's Duchy being such). This box . . . had escaped the Duke of Wellington's raid. It contained veiled references to children of the marriage though without information as to

*Anita Leslie: *Mrs Fitzherbert* (Hutchinson, 1960)

their fate. My great-grandmother enjoyed snipping out whatever might have displeased her idol, "the poor dear Queen". The Duke of Cornwall's box still resides in a cupboard, and inside it lie a mass of Maria Fitzherbert's letters and papers—all tampered with. Scissors have cut out what one most wishes to know . . . '

CHAPTER SEVEN

Foreign Visitors
in the 1820's

'Nothing lets us down more in the eyes of the English than their obse-
quious worship by foreigners; the meanness of which consists in this,
that its true foundation usually lies in the profound respect which high
and low have for English gold.'

Prinz Herman von Pückler-Muskau:
Aus den Briefen eines Verstorbenen (1830)

Whatever mazes of emotion the Prince of Wales might be treading behind
the walls of the Pavilion during the long years of his residence there, the
mere fact of his presence was enough to ensure Brighton's continuing
prosperity.

Between 1770 and 1800 the number of houses doubled. As Professor
Edmund W. Gilbert has pointed out in an admirably documented study
of the town's growth:* 'During these years the letting of lodgings to fashionable visitors became the means of livelihood for many Brightonians.
Everybody who could do so converted some part of his house into apart-
ments; Brighton became a town of lodging houses. In Brighton in 1800
there were nearly 1,300 houses, of which 211 were let solely as lodging-
houses and in another 208 lodgings were to be obtained, so that about
one-third of all the houses in the town were engaged in the business of letting lodgings.'

Building went on at an accelerated pace during the next two decades
and by 1821 there were nearly 4,000 houses, concerning which Gilbert
reminds us that 'it must not be imagined that the fine Regency buildings
built for the upper classes and the many streets of bow-windowed houses
for middle-class visitors were the only dwellings to be erected during this
period'. He points out that many back streets of small, insanitary houses

---

*Edmund W. Gilbert: *Brighton: Old Ocean's Bauble* (Flare Books, 1975)

84

were built to accommodate the army of domestics and other workers who were flocking into the town to make a living by attending to the needs of the new type of resident and visitor. This authority adds: 'The slum areas built in Brighton were in all respects as bad as those of the industrial towns of the north'.

Contemporary documents give us very little information about working-class life in Brighton; only much later, when the social conscience began to awaken in Victoria's reign, do letters, diaries and printed books begin to tell us much about what went on below the middle-middle-class. But we do get a few glimpses of the sea-going community.

I referred in the preceding chapter to the danger they ran of capture by the French during the Revolutionary and Napoleonic Wars, but they were also in peril on their own soil—from the press gang who, although they would take tinkers and tailors if they had to, naturally preferred that His Majesty's ships should be manned by experienced seamen. An Admiralty report of 1779 records that a press in that year had to report failure because the inhabitants were forewarned and 'every man kept himself locked up and bolted' for ten hours.

Again, in 1807, the *Morning Post* concluded an account of the Prince Regent's attendance at Brighton races with eight-year-old Minney Seymour as follows: '. . . by three o'clock the ground was entirely cleared, occasioned by the rain coming on, to the great disappointment of a numerous press gang, who had come on purpose to clear the town of many idle hands, in which it abounds.'

There are references to these 'idle hands' by J. C. Michell, editor of the 1829 edition of Dr Anthony Relhan's *Short History of Brighthelmston*, who indicates that because of the hardships and difficulties of their calling many of the Brighton fishermen were—by his day—drifting into alternative occupations (or none at all) as the changing character of the town offered easier money. 'That the present fishermen are different from their forefathers', he writes, 'is obvious to such natives as recollect the industrious habits and prudent manner of living of those from whom they spring. Most of them formerly supported their families without parochial relief . . .'

He goes on to describe just how hard a fisherman's life could be: 'In lamenting the degenerated morals of some of the fishermen, we cannot withhold our praise from such as still adhere to the industrious and sober examples of their father—and who continue to pursue an employment which is the best and most natural source of wealth and permanent prosperity to a maritime town. The dangers and obstructions which attend their labours are known only to themselves. It not infrequently happens that the hopes and property of the fisherman are destroyed early in the mackerel and herring season by the loss of his nets. These extend some a mile and a half, others two miles in length, and are liable to become entangled, or as it is termed 'puddened' by porpoises and dogfish, or cut asunder by large vessels pursuing their course in the dark, and so lost or rendered useless for the remainder of the season.

'They are often out for 24, occasionally for 48 hours, and more without catching fish sufficient to remunerate them for their expense, besides the loss of time. In gales of wind which have compelled ships of large burthen to seek for shelter in harbour, and in tempests which have overwhelmed stout built vessels, these hardy men have rode out the storm in their open boats, watching through the night, and labouring for the preservation of their lives and their barques—wet, and with no shelter except a small cobble or coy* in the bow of the boat, where there is scarcely room for a man to lie down in! In the severest night, their best sustenance is that of cold meat, with beer, dearly purchased at a public house . . . it cannot be a matter of surprise, although one of great regret, that the losses and hardships to which these men are exposed, break the spirit of some, and that they should abandon their original employment for other occupations, or sink into those vices which frequent visits to the gin shops and alehouses entail upon them to the utter ruin of themselves and their families.'

Written sources of this period usually tell us not about half-frozen fishermen driven to the gin-bottle, but about the gentry and those bourgeois who were prosperous or amusing enough to be accepted into their circle. But even these texts, if they are written by native authors, omit much which would interest a present-day reader. A man dealing with his own time and his own country will (unless he is deliberately writing for posterity, which is rare) leave out all the commonplaces which his contemporaries would have found boring but can help us to see his scene in the round.

It is in this respect that foreign writers are a godsend, because to them much of the familiar is unfamiliar and so worth setting down for readers in their own country. In 1827—the year the Prince left Brighton—two foreigners visited the town and subsequently wrote books; one entirely about Brighton, the other about the British Isles as a whole but with several pas-

---

*A short, flat-bottomed rowing boat

sages on Brighton. One was an Anglophile Frenchman who admired almost everything, the other a German who approved of very little.

It was still a thriving, fashionable Brighton that they saw; no one knew that the Prince had departed never to return and by now the town's progress had gained such momentum that it would probably had made little difference if they had. (In any case Mrs Fitzherbert was still there and, as Creevey said, 'she is treated as queen, at least of Brighton'.)

Between 1821 and 1831 the population swelled from 24,429 to 40,634, the highest percentage growth of any English town in those ten years; and in the same period the number of houses increased from just under 4,000 to 7,000 so that our two foreign visitors arrived in the middle of a building boom.

The Frenchman was the Comte Auguste-Louis-Charles de La Garde, a scion of the old nobility, who, as a boy, had gone into hiding during the Reign of Terror and thereafter had spent most of his life in exile, only finally returning to his native country after Napoleon's first abdication in 1814. He earned his living by writing and his best-remembered book is a gossipy account of the Congress of Vienna (the Prince de Ligne who made the remark about the 'congress dancing' was a relative of his; it was to La Garde that he made it). He visited Brighton in 1827 but his book about it did not appear until 1834: *Brighton, Scènes Détachées d'un Voyage en Angleterre*.

Prinz Herman von Pückler-Muskau, who visited Brighton a few months before La Garde (neither mentions the other), came to England to revive his flagging family fortunes by marrying an heiress. So extravagant were his tastes that he had run through not only his own inheritance but that of the Countess of Pappenheim, whom he had married in 1817. Although they were devoted to each other, they decided on a divorce of convenience and a wife-hunting expedition to England, which to nineteenth-century Europeans was a synonym for ostentatious wealth, just as the United States were to be in the first half of this century and the oil sheikhdoms in the second.

The German prince was less mercenary than he thought and could not bring himself to propose to any of the suitable prospects (one of whom was pretty Miss Gibbins of Brighton, with a fortune of £50,000). But fortunately he had provided a running commentary on the British scene in a series of letters to his deserted Countess and, when he returned to Germany, recouped his finances by concocting a book from an edited version of this correspondence. It was an immediate success all over Europe and in America, mainly on account of its witty derision of the English, who were as unpopular as the most successful nationals of any particular period usually are. The German version, *Aus den Briefen eines Verstorbenen* (Letters from a Dead Man), appeared in 1830 and a slightly abridged and occasionally bowdlerised version in English in 1832.*

La Garde arrived on one of the paddle-steamers that ran twice a week between Brighton and Dieppe and 'drew in alongside a pier, a kind of bridge suspended on chains—a model of grace combined with solidity that was a worthy introduction to the magnificent amphitheatre behind it.' The *'espèce de pont'* was the famous Chain Pier, completed in 1823. It was the brain-child of a retired naval officer, Captain Samuel Brown, who patented a method of constructing suspension bridges which he subsequently applied to piers; some of his ideas were incorporated by Telford in his bridge across the Menai Straits. (As Brighton has no natural harbour, the pier was to suffer much damage from storms and was finally destroyed in 1896.)

The Frenchman had a bad crossing. In good weather this usually took 12 hours but a gale kept him at sea for 24 and he suffered the 'agonies which bruise every limb as if one had been stretched on the rack'.

However he recovered sufficiently to make a good meal on his arrival at the Gloucester Hotel in Gloucester Place (which still exists as a public house). He recommended this establishment to any other traveller seeking 'a polite hostess, attentive servants and—a much greater rarity in Brighton—moderate prices'.

He continued in this enthusiastic vein: 'An admirable dinner was set before me, consisting of the excellent fish which abound in Brighton; mutton said to be the best in all England—because the Downs on which the flocks feed are impregnated with salt; tasty vegetables—even though they *had* been boiled; a variety of puddings; and some Portuguese wines—just a shade too heavy for my palate.

'I was quite ready for bed by the time I had completed my meal and perused some newspapers . . . The Boots presented me and every other guest with a boot-jack and slippers; then, candle in hand, he took me up to my room where my luggage had been deposited carefully. I should perhaps explain that "Boots" is the title given to the hotel servant whose special task it is to look after boots and shoes. Nowhere in England does one find a Jack-of-all-work. Each servant has specific duties and will do no other.

---

*The original nineteenth-century translation is available in a modern edition, edited with an intoduction by E. M. Butler: *A Regency Visitor—The English Tour of Prince Pückler-Muskau* (Collins, 1957)

'The staircase, although small, was elegant and carpeted. The comfortable bed was of a size that would have accommodated at least three travellers in a German hostelry. Four carved pillars of massive mahogany supported the tastefully draped tester. The bedding consisted of an enormous pile of mattresses surmounted by a thick feather-bed. When I had scaled this peaceful fortress (with the aid of a small flight of steps) and drawn its double curtains of white muslin, I found myself installed in something like an inner room, at least as spacious as a monk's cell. In safe haven and in lively anticipation of the novel scenes I was about to witness, I had no trouble in sinking into a deep sleep and putting behind me all the fatigues and nausea of that short sea-crossing.'

Awaking to a sunny morning which sustains his good humour, he examines and records for our benefit the furnishings of a Brighton hotel, which, although of a good middling sort, was certainly not one of the most luxurious and expensive.

'Its studied neatness was a delight to the eye', he writes. 'A soft carpet covers the floor at all seasons of the year. A marble fireplace, extending only a short way into the room, is decorated with a number of graceful little trinkets. The fire-irons have such a polish that they are obviously cleaned every day. The iron grate, a foot high, is filled with coal as black and shining as jet. As to the furnishing, there is a toilet table set out with everything necessary for one's morning ablutions: such as basins of all sizes and for a variety of purposes (in porcelain or Wedgwood ware); crystal bottles; face- and hand-towels in linen or cotton; perfumed Windsor soap. And all this in the bedroom of an inn!'

Brighton had come a long way from the semi-troglodyte lodgings of the Rev. William Clarke less than a century before.

He then refers to a detail of behaviour which was always a pleasant surprise to visitors from the Continent. 'I was hardly awake when a trim maidservant brought me hot water and took my order for breakfast. This was when I first noticed a very convenient custom which obtains here. Even if you ring for them a score of times, the servants never come into your room without first knocking.' (English tourists in Europe at this period were always embarrassed and often angry at the way hotel servants burst into their bedrooms without warning, regardless of the guest's sex, state of undress or occupation.)

Even Pückler-Muskau had a good word for English inn servants. 'If you want anything, the sound of your bell brings either a neatly-dressed maidservant, with a respectful curtsey, or a smart well-dressed waiter, who receives your orders in the garb and with the air of an adroit valet; instead of an uncombed lad, in short jacket and green apron, who asks you with a mixture of stupidity and insolence: "Was schaffen's Ihr Gnoden?" [What is it your Honour?] or "Haben *Sie* hier jeklingelt?" [Was it *you*, here, that rang?] and then runs out again without understanding properly what is wanted.'

La Garde was fortunate in meeting, the day after his arrival, General Sir Robert Wilson, who lived at No. 72, King's Road, the new carriage road along the sea-front which had been completed only five years before.

Sir Robert was a somewhat unconventional soldier who, in the Peninsula, had commanded the Loyal Lusitanian Legion, a body of Portuguese troops under British officers, and later served as a liaison officer with the Russian, Austrian and Prussian armies in Eastern Europe. He was frequently in disgrace with 'the Establishment', the exploit which earned most official displeasure being a Scarlet Pimpernel episode in Paris where, in 1814, he helped Count Lavalette to escape from a Bourbon prison. However, he had the entrée to Brighton's world of fashion and so could provide La Garde with the introductions he needed if he was to find readable 'copy' for his book.

La Garde—very usefully—gives us a foreigner's first impressions of Brighton at a time when most of its 'Regency' architecture (George IV had been on the throne since 1820) was brand-new or still being built.

Much of what he saw was the work of three men who, a reliable authority tells us, built 'four—possibly five—squares, four crescents, nine terraces, six streets, five churches, a large number of individual private houses, and in addition were no doubt responsible for other buildings no trace of their connection with which has been preserved'.*

They were Amon Wilds and Amon Henry Wilds—father and son—and Charles Augustus (or Augustin) Busby.

Amon Wilds the elder was originally a builder in Lewes and it was there that he first adopted a decorative device which he and his son later used as a 'signature' on many of their buildings. In 1819 he converted two houses in Castle Place, Lewes High Street, into one. His client was Dr Gideon Mantell, a pioneer geologist, and—either for this reason or as a visual pun on his own name—Wilds used 'ammonite' capitals on the pilasters of the façade. The incorporation of a design based on this fossil was not his invention (it had been used by George Dance in Pall Mall, London, 30

---

*Antony Dale: *Fashionable Brighton, 1820–1860* (Oriel Press Limited, 1967)

years earlier) but obviously tickled his fancy for he and his son were to repeat it on many of their buildings in Brighton to which they had migrated in 1815.

His son, Amon Henry Wilds, who in later life is said to have received commissions from as far afield as Wales and Ireland, styled himself an architect whereas his father remained content with the appellation of builder (in any case the two callings were then less separate than they have since become).

Busby, grandson of a coach-painter and son of a musician, studied at the Royal Academy's school of drawing and exhibited a 'Design for a Mansion' there when he was only 13. At 19 he published his first book, *A Series of Designs for Villas and Country Houses adapted with Economy to the Comforts and to the Elegancies of Modern Life, with Plans and Explanations to Each.* Rejecting the style of the Adam brothers—whom he accused of a 'depravity of taste' inherited from the Romans—he asserted that it was only in the simpler forms of Ancient Greece that he could find models of the necessary elegance.

After publishing another book and executing a number of commissions in this country he visited the United States, where his interests—for reasons which no surviving written record explains—included paddle steamers and penitentiaries. He published an article on marine propulsion in the *American Monthly Magazine* of June, 1818, and inspected state prisons in Massachusetts, Connecticut, New Jersey, Pennsylvania, Maryland and Virginia.

He returned to England in 1821 and a year later established himself in Brighton, where he went into partnership with Amon Wilds senior. A. H. Wilds was possibly part of this arrangement but probably not. There are indications that he worked on his own account as an architect, although he and his father may have continued to operate together in the construction business.

In the late 1700's most of the housing development in Brighton had been to the north of the town and just immediately east of the Steine. The forerunner of the subsequent spread along the coastline had been Royal Crescent, 14 'elegant lodging houses' built in isolation on the cliffs by J. B. Otto, a West Indian speculator, in 1808. But the intervening space soon filled up and by 1818 nearly half Brighton's houses were east of the Steine. In 1827 when La Garde arrived, still further extensions were being made, both of an architectural quality that was to endear them to posterity: Kemp Town to the east and Brunswick Town to the west.

The design for the former was the first assignment of the Wilds and Busby partnership and their plans for the Brunswick estate (perhaps entirely Busby's work) followed only a year later.

La Garde, no country cousin but a seasoned traveller familiar with most of the European capitals, was an interested—and admiring— observer of this changed and still changing Brighton.

'The width of the streets', he wrote, 'the granite pavements which assure the safety of pedestrians on both sides of the road, the elegance of the larger and of even quite unpretentious houses, all this told one—even at a cursory glance—that Brighton is a resort entirely dedicated to the world of fashion. The close proximity of London (for one can speak of proximity when public coaches will cover the distance in five hours) makes Brighton an elegant epitome of the metropolis. It has the same luxury, the same glitter, but without that rush of business which in London seems to allow neither place nor time for private pleasures. There are shops in rich variety. Those selling fruit, fish and meat are chiefly remarkable for an exquisite cleanliness which one could well wish to see copied elsewhere. The shopmen seem to be at pains to avoid offending any of the other senses in an environment where the palate should be one's sole counsellor . . .

'In front of many of the houses there are vivid green lawns and little gardens of flowers. The large windows are nearly always open (for the English love fresh air and do not mind being seen), so that one is able to look into their houses and observe that luxury and convenience of furnishing which can only be described by their word, "comfort". But that which I like above all is the "veranda", a sort of iron trellis work in various designs which projects from each floor like a balcony and is surmounted by a zinc "tent", striped in different colours. Over most of them rambler-roses or other climbing plants are trained, seeming to transport the onlooker to some tropic clime and giving to the houses of Brighton the indolent gaiety of the Indies. Everything about these dwellings seems designed for people who will go on enjoying them, undisturbed, for ever. Yet, in fact, their occupants are the merest birds-of-passage!'

Walking along the sea-front he enjoyed 'the spectacle of the succession of squares built round lawns or gardens of flowers and shrubs' and went on to further encomiums of what is still one of Brighton's greatest charms: 'It is an excellent idea to create these precincts—variously called Squares, Crescents or Circuses—which provide a pleasant alternative to what would otherwise be a monotonous march of buildings. Each of the gardens is enclosed by an iron fence and only the occupants of the neighbouring houses have the key of the gate and the right of entry. A Parisian hearing descriptions of the charms of the squares in English towns probably does not realise that the old Place-Royal can give him only the faintest notion of what can be achieved in London and Brighton.'

An 'infinite' number of houses, he said, were rising 'as if by magic': 'I entered several houses where the builders were still at work. I noticed, not for the first time, that all the houses—whether large or small—were built to exactly the same plan; only the scale was different. Thus, there is no *porte-cochère*. Quite a small doorway leads into a hall from which one enters a parlour that also serves as a dining-room. A narrow staircase leads to the first floor where there are two *salons*, one large and one small. On the second floor are the bedrooms of the family. The servants sleep in the attics and the kitchens are in the basement. On the outside there is a similar uniformity. There are never more than three sash-windows in the front of the house (the reason for this is the window-tax, which people seek every possible means of evading). But by joining several of these houses together into an integral unity, it becomes possible to decorate them richly with architectural features borrowed from Greece, Rome or Asia. This is the device which produces the "palaces" that the stranger finds so astonishing.

'Not long ago the only building material known in England was brick (stone, because it is so expensive, was reserved solely for public buildings). Blackened by smoke and fogs, the brick soon took on a grubby appearance very depressing to contemplate. But, a few years since, the discovery of Roman cement began to give an entirely new look to British building. The brick, fashioned into pillars, capitals and pediments, is completely coated with the cement which lends itself to the most delicate kind of ornament. Perfectly hardened by contact with the air and then carefully whitened, it could easily be taken for Genoan or Florentine marble.'

He adds: 'The rents of these houses are often fantastically high and during the season the weekly rent for a house in Brighton would enable you to take a veritable mansion for a whole year in France.'

Probably as a result of an introduction from Sir Robert Wilson, La Garde was invited to dine with a man whose name is still borne by one of the most architecturally notable quarters of Brighton: Kemp Town.

'Like most famous cities', says La Garde, 'Kemp Town bears the name of its founder. In France and most other countries, a man builds one house, possibly two or three. Mr Kemp, a man with immense capital resources at his command, conveived the idea of building an entire town and has achieved it. It is a noble conception to link one's name with an enterprise which, in succeeding ages can say: Te Saxa Loquuntur—Our Very Stones Speak of You.'

Thomas Read Kemp was one of the lords of the manor of Brighton, and for many years M.P. for the county town of Lewes where his family had been established since the middle of the eighteenth century. On his marriage to a daughter of Sir Francis Baring, chairman of the East India Company and founder of the great banking firm of Baring Brothers, his father settled on him Sussex properties worth £20,000. Sir Francis gave his daughter £10,000 and an undertaking that she should receive a similar sum on his death. In 1811 Kemp inherited the whole of the family fortune except £10,000 settled on his sister and 12 years later he began the great enterprise that was to make his name and ruin him.

His basic idea, a good one, was that the houses then existing or being built in Brighton were, although elegant, not large enough to appeal to the really affluent and that he would find many buyers of this class if he built—in open country on the cliffs to the east of Brighton—a well laid-out estate of houses similar to those Nash was building in London.

Kemp Town was still being built when La Garde visited it and in fact the estate as its creator envisaged it was never completed. What he did build is sufficiently impressive and is still there for us to see. Its centre, Sussex Square, is larger than Grosvenor Square in London and leads into a magnificent crescent whose diameter (840 feet) is 200 feet greater than that of the Royal Crescent at Bath. As originally planned Kemp Town would have been twice the size it is, but the scheme was too grandiose even for Kemp's considerable fortune and in 1837, like so many unfortunates of fact and fiction at this time, he was in such financial trouble that he had to flee to France. He died in Paris in 1844 and was buried in the cemetery of Père-la-Chaise.

His obituary in the *Gentleman's Magazine* concluded with this cold comfort to the author of 'one of the most magnificent assemblages of private dwellings in the kingdom': 'Mr. Kemp was ruined by this gigantic speculation, though now the property must be of immense value.'

La Garde (and presumably Kemp) had no inkling of this dark future when a lavish dinner party at No. 22 Sussex Square enabled the Frenchman to observe some of our tribal customs.

'A whole regiment of servants in rich livery awaited to receive me on the steps and in the vestibule . . . My name, which I gave at the door, had been announced four times by the time I reached the drawing room! According to the English code of manners, I was presented to each of the guests, whose names were recited to me. From the moment of this formality—which places a great strain on the memory!— one is permitted to address one's neighbours at table. Without this piece of protocol any converse with them would have been unthinkable, even if one had seen them a dozen times before.'

In the dining room he was overcome with admiration of the silver dinner service and the crested plate on the sideboard. He recorded his dislike of turtle soup which he took to be 'fashionable merely because it is expensive' and then went on to express astonishment at the eating preferences of the majority of his English fellow-guests.

'The dinner, prepared by a French chef, comprised a great many dishes, all of them prepared with consummate skill. However, such is the force of habit (or dare I say prejudice?) that none of the guests—apart from the foreigners among them or those English who had spent a good deal of time abroad—touched any dish that was the least bit unorthodox by their national standards. While some of us were relishing poultry, game and fish dressed and seasoned in the French mode, the ruggedly insular guests—those whom one may term the true indigenous puritans—stuck scrupulously to roast beef or to fish and vegetables that had been boiled. It should be noticed, however, that this stoicism of theirs imposes on them burdens which they could otherwise avoid and demands at the same time a certain amount of culinary expertise which, logically speaking, accords ill with their Spartan pretensions. For the fact is that when the vegetables or the fish have been put on the table just as they emerged from their pan of boiling water, each of these ultra-English Englishmen has to manufacture a sauce of his own! To this end he is provided with a collection of glass bottles containing pimento, Cayenne pepper and every sort of spice (even seasonings imported ready-made from the Indies): in a word, a very gourmand's laboratory. To me it seems most odd that one should bring expert cooks great distances and at enormous expense and then make one's own sauce—at the table!'

He was equally astonished that champagne which in other countries was 'usually introduced to enliven the end of the meal when the guests are somewhat replete' was drunk throughout until replaced by claret as the dessert was served. Both were 'in profusion and of the best' because, said La Garde, 'since the exorbitant customs duties affect equally the good and the mediocre product, the English import only the best'.

When the ladies withdrew he remarked to his neighbour that he hoped the gentlemen would not sit drinking for several hours, since 'a table without women is a garden without flowers'.

The Englishman (all La Garde tells us about him is that his name was Marshall) seems to have regarded this implied criticism of his country as a typical piece of foreign impertinence. 'It is our custom', he replied stiffly, 'and when you say *that* in England there is no second opinion and no argument. We hold to custom like a snail to its shell.' Then relenting a little, 'However, I must admit that our habits are beginning to be modified a little in this regard.'

And, to La Garde's relief, this was the case that evening: 'When the ladies had left us the cloth was taken off, revealing a magnificent mahogany table on which glasses were set and around which choice wines circulated with some rapidity in crystal decanters mounted on little four-wheeled carriages made of silver. As I have indicated, in former times—and even now in circles where custom dies hard—one used to drink until the early hours of the morning; but our libations lasted no longer than an hour and we went up to the drawing-room as soon as coffee was announced.'

He was moved to other comments on 'the dining habits of the English' when Sir Robert took him to meet one of his old comrades-in-arms, Colonel Black.

'Fresh plates are provided for each course', he noted, 'and fresh silver utensils for each dish. It did seem to me, however, unnecessarily wearisome for the host and hostess that etiquette demanded that they themselves should serve the fish and carve the poultry and joints, thus debarring them completely from joining in the conversation with their guests. It would suit hosts and guests a good deal better if this tiresome chore were left to the servants, as it is in all other countries nowadays . . .

'A custom generally followed during the meal generates considerable cordiality and cameraderie among the guests. Everyone is called upon repeatedly to pledge a toast proposed by one of the others. When he hears his name (or is alerted by one of the servants if he is sitting too far away), he waits for you to tell him the choice of wine; the glasses are filled; you nod to him; he nods back; and you both drink. I had my fair share of these toasts. It is perhaps a little annoying for the ladies that they cannot drink until someone else proposes their health, but English gallantry ensures that they do not suffer on this account.'

After the ladies had withdrawn he observed with some distaste an English custom which required the production of a chamber-pot from the sideboard.

'I will say no more than one word about the usage which permits all the gentlemen to retire, one after the other, to a corner of the room—an old-fashioned procedure that rather conflicts with the delicacy of modern manners. What appears to me even more strange is their invariable habit of drinking the health of the guest who is momentarily away from the table. As what he is doing does not prevent his hearing what is said, he is able to prepare a short speech of reply, which he delivers with due gravity before resuming his place at the table.'

Another oddity on which he seized as a collector's item came to his notice when Sir Robert took him to call on Lady Hotham at No. 55 Brunswick Square.

'On arrival I was astounded at the veritable tattoo which he beat on the door with the brass knocker. I did not yet know that each class of society has a different manner of knocking on a door. Sir Robert noticed my amazement.

' "Rather different", he chuckled, "from the gentle taps you give in Paris!" and continued: "You should be aware of certain subtle nuances in English etiquette and, as they say, seeing is believing. Thus: the postman knocks twice; ordinary folk three times; those of higher degree seven, eight or even nine times in quick succession. As for tradesmen they are only allowed to knock once and the servants of the house do not knock at all—they ring the bell." '

Equally remarkable to the French visitor was the intrepidity of the English in plunging into their northern sea as late as October. He describes the procedure: 'A hut on wheels was provided with everything that was needed after and during the bathe, such as towels, flannels and so on. The bather got in. The attendant climbed on a kind of seat and drove the hut down the beach until it was in a sufficient depth of water. Then he turned the horse round to face up the beach again, thus enabling the bather to enter the sea very conveniently by a little ladder at the back of the hut. If a lady or child required just a simple dip, two females seized them by the arms as they emerged from the hut and plunged them in the water three times. The English ascribe considerable virtue to the electric shock administered to the limbs by this sudden immersion in cold salt water.'

La Garde was full of praise for the fact that in England—or at least in

Brighton—'to-day everyone hastens to speak to a Frenchman in his own tongue, to a point where they positively discourage him from talking English. This is certainly true among the upper classes and, to some extent, in the middle-class'. (Pückler-Muskau, however, poked fun at an English-woman who insisted on speaking nothing but French to him during his voyage to England. Describing her personal formula for avoiding sea-sickness, she said that at the first signs of a rough sea she would gather together all the mattresses and blankets she could find and cocoon herself in her bunk. A cure that never failed, she claimed, was to sleep between two *matelots*.)

There is considerable contrast between their descriptions of what a ball in Brighton was like in 1827. La Garde tells us he is describing such an event at the 'Old Ship'; Pückler-Muskau does not specify the venue but his mention of a staircase suggests that he, too, is speaking of the Ship.

'The prosaic ball', he writes, 'so little answered my expectations that I was perfectly astonished. A narrow staircase led directly into the ball-room, which was ill-lighted and miserably furnished, and surrounded with worsted cords to divide the dancers from the spectators. An orchestra for the musicians was hung with ill-washed white draperies, which looked like sheets hung out to dry. Imagine a second room near it, with benches along the walls, and a large tea-table in the middle; in both rooms the numerous company raven black from head to foot, gloves inclusive; a melancholy style of dancing, without the least trace of vivacity or joy-ousness; so that the only feeling you have is that of compassion for the use-less fatigue the poor people are enduring . . .'

Now La Garde: 'Although the ball was given in an hotel (or what we should call a tavern) I was dazzled at my entry by the profusion of lights, the richness of the costumes and the brilliance of the decorations. The ladies were dressed in the height of fashion and plentifully adorned with diamonds and other precious stones. They may have lacked something of that piquant *chic* which one finds to perfection only in the Parisienne, but in compensation there was such a freshness of colouring, such a cast of fea-ture and virginal expression that they might have stepped from some delicious canvas of Raphael or Correggio . . . The dancers were per-forming a "Reel", a Scottish dance, consisting of most graceful postures and demanding an extraordinary agility if it is to be well done. I find it paradoxical that our traditionally phlegmatic neighbours should so enjoy a measure that is a good deal brisker and more sprightly than the Neapoli-tan tarantella.'

Pückler-Muskau complains that ballrooms in Brighton are stiflingly overcrowded: '. . . in rooms to which a respectable German citizen would not venture to invite twelve people, some hundreds are here packed like negro slaves. It is even worse than in London; and the space allotted to the quadrilles allows only the mathematical possibility of something like dancing demonstrations. A ball without this crowd would be despised; and a visitor of any fashion who found the staircase empty would say of a rout, "Si j'y entre, je n'y vais pas" (if I can get in, I shan't go).'

Madame de Staël had expressed similar views about British ballrooms. 'You are as rudely jostled', she said, 'as you would be in the pit of a theatre and only the most robust can venture into one of their *salons* without being suffocated.'

It was she that La Garde was refuting when he wrote: 'To this pre-judical view of such a celebrated woman I can only oppose my personal observation. I have attended a great many such assemblies in England and have never felt the lack of sufficient elbow-room to admire the beauties who were present. Nor have I ever been so jammed and crushed that I was unable to enjoy the delights of converse with several of my fellow-guests. . . . I have never been called upon to exert brute force in order to emerge safe and sound; and on no occasion has the thought crossed my mind that I was in any danger of asphyxiation.' (Did he 'pro-test too much'; or was this a rare—possibly unique—attempt at humour by La Garde?)

Pückler-Muskau found some consolation for the overcrowding of which he was otherwise so critical because it meant that, willy-nilly (and his tastes were such that he certainly wanted it), he was squeezed against 'a greater number of pretty girls'. They and landscape gardening were his twin enthusiasms.

CHAPTER EIGHT

Victorian Brighton

'It has been alleged that the being wafted through the air at the rate of twenty or thirty miles an hour must affect delicate lungs and asthmatic people; that to such as are of sanguineous constitution and labour under fulness of blood in the head the movement of rail trains will produce apoplexy; that the sudden plunging into the darkness of a tunnel and the emerging out of it as suddenly cannot fail to make work for the oculists; and, finally, it has never been doubted but that the air in such tunnels is of a vitiated kind and must give rise to the worst effects; while that at the bottom of deep cuttings or excavations, being necessarily damp, will occasion catarrhs and multiply agues.'

A. B. Granville: *The Spas of England* (1841)

For the greater part of Brighton's history to travel there from London or any other place north of the Downs has been discouragingly difficult. By the fifteenth century the hard-surfaced roads which the Romans had built for the crossing of the Weald were quite worn out—and thereafter the sticky mud of Sussex became notorious. Dr John Burton, from whose journal of a visit to the county in the first half of the eighteenth century I quoted earlier, asked his readers: 'Why is it that the oxen, the swine, the women and all other animals are so long-legged in Sussex? May it be from the difficulty of pulling the feet out of so much mud by the strength of the ankle that the muscles get stretched, as it were, and the bones lengthened?'

In his day it still took two days to travel from London to Brighton by carrier's wagon; a private carriage could cover the distance in a day if all went well (Charles II's carriage had overturned 12 times between his leaving Whitehall and arriving at the Duke of Northumberland's country house in Petworth).

The introduction of Royal Mail coaches by John Palmer in 1784 and John Macadam's announcement to Parliament of a new method of road-making in 1811 both contributed to an improvement in the surfaces and consequent refinement in the design of vehicles. By the time the

Comte de La Garde travelled from Brighton to London early in 1828 there were 24 coaches in each direction every day. The journey took him only seven hours and he speaks of 'a road as smooth and well-gravelled as a garden path'.

He had been on the point of hiring a post-chaise for the journey when a friend recommended a stage-coach on the grounds of economy and because—as 'an avowed observer of our nation'—he would have the advantage of 'meeting those "characters" that are to be found in the public vehicles of any country'.

He had no reason to regret this decision when the coach pulled up at the Gloucester: 'As soon as I saw it I knew it would have been pure vanity to have travelled post. The horses and their harness and the vehicle itself were of such elegance that a Margrave of Bayreuth or Anspach might well have coveted the whole turn-out for state occasions. To complete the illusion, a fanfare on the posthorn was performed with considerable *panache* by the guard sitting at the back of the coach. His instrument, far more harmonious than the little trumpets of German postillions, awoke a musical echo in the spacious streets through which we passed and soon we were speeding in full career beyond the boundaries of Brighton'.

La Garde rode inside, but most of his fellow travellers, 'among whom were several ladies', preferred the half-price seats and the fresh air on top of the vehicle: 'A long ladder was placed against the side of the coach so that they could climb to the roof. But their troubles were not over when they had made this perilous escalade. Their mode of travelling demanded a certain expertness (and the absence of any tendency to vertigo!) for, once perched aloft, they had to keep their balance at all times—even when asleep. It is the passengers at each end of the benches who are particularly called upon to concentrate on their situation. The end of each bench projects somewhat beyond the body of the coach and ends in an iron handrail only a few inches high. Often no more than half the passenger's body is supported by the seat; the other half is suspended in space. When the coach is careering along at full speed one can often see a terrified novice traveller clinging to one end of a seat in a rigid state of terror while at the other end the habitué balances himself with all the insouciance of a sailor on a yardarm.'

An even speedier form of travel was to be the third of the stimuli prompting Brighton to yet further growth (from 40,600 inhabitants in 1831 to 90,000 in 1871). Dr Russell and his book on the virtues of sea-water had been the first; the Prince Regent and his Pavilion the second;

the third was to be the railway—more than compensating for the new and unwelcome phenomenon of Royal disapproval.

George IV died in 1830, to be succeeded by his elderly and eccentric brother, 'Silly Billy'. William IV was a frequent though less flamboyant visitor than George, but Victoria—who came to the throne in 1837—soon decided that Brighton stood high on the list of places, individuals and opinions that did not amuse her; and she was never one to be reticent or half-hearted about her displeasure.

According to *Punch* she found its people 'a set of unmannerly curs that poke their noses under the bonnet of a Queen'. The kind of behaviour that annoyed her and (in her own words) made the place 'quite a prison' was reported in the *Sunday Times* of 9 February 1845:

'Brighton, February 8th. This morning, at nine o'clock, her Majesty and Prince Albert, without any attendants, left the Castle Square entrance of the Palace, and walked to the Chain Pier, entirely unobserved, till they were about to return . . . As the royal pair were leaving the pier, about 200 persons who had congregated on the Marine-parade ran forward so as to head them in their passing through the toll-gate. From this spot to the Palace is somewhat more than 100 yards, and while this space was being traversed by royalty some curious and impertinent visitors (we have never recognised among the parties who have thus acted any of the *inhabitants* of Brighton) pressed round her Majesty and her royal consort, some of them even pressing beneath the royal bonnet . . . This annoyance to the Queen is a disgrace to the town. The persons who surrounded the Queen were chiefly trademen's boys . . . with baskets on their arms, and the tradesmen ought to know that such conduct on the part of their servants would be likely to drive her Majesty from the town, and deprive them from the advantage of her occasional residence at the Pavilion'.

Drive her it did. She left Brighton that month and did not return for 20 years.

She had been unwise to attempt a 'walkabout' as late as 1845 if crowds annoyed her. In 1841 a journalist could still the various classes of visitor and their preferred times of year very succinctly: 'The summer months are abandoned to the trading population of London; the early autumn is surrendered to the lawyers; and, when November summons *them* to Westminster, the *beau monde* commence their migration to encounter the gales of that inclement season secure from any participation of the pleasure with a plebeian multitude'.*

But in that same year, 1841, a development came that was to multiply the number of the *plebs* immeasurably and thereby, no doubt, to hasten the departure of the Queen.

Brighton was among the first towns to enjoy the benefits of travel on a railway. George Stephenson had invented the locomotive steam engine (to carry coals at three miles an hour) in 1814 and the first railway of any length had been suggested as early as 1818, but Parliament had rejected the proposal, one objection being that the line would pass too near a duke's fox-coverts. Three years later, however, it did authorise the Stockton-Darlington Railway and this was opened in 1825. But it was not until the inauguration of the Liverpool and Manchester Railway in 1829—in the presence of the Duke of Wellington—that this new means of transport attracted serious attention.

Yet already (in 1825) a Brighton town meeting had passed a resolution in favour of a railway that could transport coal from the adjacent port of Shoreham, thus obviating the necessity of the coal ships unloading their cargoes on to Brighton beach and offending the more fastidious bathers by depositing a gritty black scum on the surface of the sea. This, for the time being, came to nothing, as did the proposal by a nationally famous engineer, John Rennie, to build a line from London to Bristol by way of Brighton.

A number of schemes for a London to Brighton line were put to Parliament in 1835, 1836 and 1837 and finally one drafted by Rennie, which took the most direct route and provided for branch lines to the county town of Lewes and the ports of Shoreham and Newhaven, was the one cosen. Work began in July 1838, well ahead of the 'railway mania' that was to sweep England in the 'forties as violently as the South Sea Bubble had done a century before.

The route necessitated massive engineering work including five tunnels. The most formidable of these were the one through the chalk of the North Downs at Merstham—1,830 yards long—and the Clayton Tunnel that pierces the South Downs five miles north of the terminus and is 2,266 yards long. There were also 99 bridges under and over the railway and a 37-arch viaduct to carry the line at a height of 100 feet over the valley of the Ouse south of Balcombe.

*New Monthly Magazine (1841)

A contemporary print shows us what such a project looked like in the days before bulldozers and mechanical diggers, when it was all pick, shovel and wheelbarrow work and, for most purposes, the only horse-power was the four-legged sort. Hundreds of men swarm in a deep chalk-cutting that looks far beyond the powers of such ant-like creatures.

Terry Coleman tells us how it was done in his book, *The Railway Navvies*:* 'Sometimes, when there was no use for the soil, it had to be lifted up the sloping walls of the cutting and dumped at the sides. This was done by barrow runs, and this "making the running" was the most spectacular part of navvy work, and one of the most dangerous. The runs were made by laying planks up the side of the cutting, up which barrows were wheeled. The running was performed by the strongest of the men. A rope attached to the barrow and also to each man's belt, ran up the side of the cutting, and then round a pulley at the top, where it was attached to a horse. When the barrow was loaded, a signal was given to the horse-driver at the top, and the man was drawn up the side of the cutting, balancing the barrow in front of him. If the horse pulled steadily and the man kept his balance, everything went well. The man tipped his barrow-load on top of the cutting, turned round, and went down the side of the cutting again, this time drawing his barrow after him and with his back to it, while the horse all the time kept the rope taut and took most of the weight of the empty barrow.'

By 1840 there were 6,206 men, aided by 960 horses and five locomotives, doing work as skilled and hazardous as this to make the line to Brighton.

The achievements of the 'navvy' were extraordinary but this was no body of ordinary men that cut these great gashes through the countryside. They were the 'land-navigators' who had come into being originally to construct the new network of canals in the second half of the eighteenth century. Now, recruited in even greater numbers, these nomad swarms were to provide Britain with 5,000 miles of railway track in 20 years.

They had that clannishness, that arrogant pride in their work and contempt for everyone outside their 'mystery' so often found in men of a trade which entails their moving in large bodies from place to place and never staying anywhere long enough to be accepted by the local community.

They earned at least twice as much as ordinary labourers, whom they looked down upon as a lesser breed. For this they would do back-breaking

---

*Pelican, 1976

work for 70 hours a week or more, often in conditions in which—as one of them said—'every day nearly there's an accident and nigh every week at furthest a death'. Whether English, Welsh, Scottish or Irish by birth they all attained such standards of strength and dexterity (and hence speed of working) that it was worth the while of British contractors to ship whole gangs of them abroad—instead of using cheaper local labour—when we began building railways for other countries: first, the line from Paris to Rouen, then in other parts of Europe and finally all over the world.

But they had other, less desirable, traits which must have made them as welcome as the Huns of Attila to the quiet Sussex countryfolk on their line of march. To begin with it was their practice to vary their normal diet of bread, beef and beer by poaching the preserves of local landowners and raiding the farmers' henhouses and orchards. Then, once a month, when they were given their pay, they downed tools and descended on the nearest town and village for a 'randy'—defined to an enquiring M.P. as 'a drunken frolic . . . which not uncommonly terminates in a serious fight'. The muscles of their trade made them formidable opponents and at their approach most local inhabitants (except the innkeepers) would retire behind locked doors. Such forces of law and order as existed at that time usually gave the navvy best. As one witness told the Select Committee on Railway Labourers in 1846: 'From being long known to each other they generally act in concert, and put at defiance any local constabulary force; consequently crimes of the most atrocious character are common, and robbery without attempt at concealment an everyday occurrence.'*

From such causes there was probably a strong element of 'for this relief much thanks . . .' in the enthusiasm with which the people of Brighton and its hinterland greeted the offical opening of the London to Brighton line on 21 September 1841; but nevertheless the *Brighton Herald* report of that afternoon's proceedings conveys much the same level of excitement as that with which our generation watched the first man landing on the moon.

'Parties of ladies and gentlemen were formed on every brow, and every field and meadow, from Preston to Withdean and Patcham, had its mass of human life. It was along these elevated points, which look down on the railroad, that the approach of the train was first perceived, and at about twenty minutes after twelve it was announced to those from whose sight it was yet hid by the winding of the hills by a thousand cries of "Here they

---

*Quoted in *The Victorian Underworld* by Kellow Chesney (Pelican, 1974)

come!" The first indication was a cloud of steam that poured forth from the mouth of Patcham tunnel and the next moment a long dark object was seen swiftly gliding along the line and rapidly increasing in size and distinctness as it approached, till, after being lost for a short time behind a curve, the first train from the metropolis came thundering along, and, receiving the hearty salutations of the crowds on the hills as it passed, rattled over the viaduct, and passed the engine house, and was lost to the sight of the external spectators as it turned round the rails to reach the terminus.'

This exciting new form of transport was, initially, no more comfortable than the stage-coach—probably less so. Macaulay, the historian, was no lover of trains although this did not deter him from using them. In 1843 he travelled from London to Paris by way of Brighton (a journey of 20¾ hours for a fare of 59s 6d) and on arrival at his destination complained in a letter to his sister: 'Groan One—The Brighton Railway; in a slow train, a carriage crowded as full as it would hold, a sick lady smelling of aether, a healthy gentleman smelling of brandy, the thermometer 102° in the shade, and I not in the shade, but exposed to the full glare of the sun from noon till after two, the effect of which is that my white trousers have been scorched into a pair of very serviceable nankeens' (i.e. to a buff colour).

Despite his 'groan', Macaulay probably travelled first-class (an enclosed coach with padded seats) or just possibly second (enclosed with hard seats), but less prosperous passengers would go third (open sides but with a roof), or fourth (not even a roof).

The railway superseded the stage coach relentlessly and with astonishing speed, in spite of the discomforts described by Macaulay and the fact that—only a month after the opening—a train ran off the line 12 miles north of Brighton, killing two passengers.* In 1835 there had been 23 coaches leaving Brighton for London every day. By the end of 1841 there were only four; two years later only one. It was not novelty alone that brought about the change, but the two basic factors of travel economics: speed and price. The coach took five hours to reach London; the train did the journey in two. An outside seat on the coach cost 13s; a second-class ticket on the train 9s 6d.

The volume of traffic was swollen to unprecedented proportions by the introduction of cheap-day excursion trains in 1844. In 1845 a third-class Sunday excursion return ticket cost 5s; in 1849, 3s 6d; in 1861, 2s 6d. In

---

*Twenty years later a disaster in Clayton Tunnel killed 23 people and injured 175.

the whole of 1837 the coaches had carried 50,000 passengers to Brighton; during the summer of 1850 the railway often carried half as many again *in a single week.*

By 1861 it was estimated that the annual number of visitors was a quarter of a million and on one day in 1862—Easter Monday—the trains carried 132,000 passengers to the town. In what respects did the new type of visitor—particularly the Cockney tripper of the excursion train—change the scene? Fortunately there was one skilled and eloquent observer to tell us. Richard Jefferies is now best remembered as a naturalist but he was also interested in recording the habits of the human species. His book, *The Open Air*, which contains a description of Brighton beach, was not published until 1885, but it is fair to assume that it was equally applicable in 1861 or 1862, and probably in the 1840's.

It presents a picture far less sedate than that made famous by W. P. Frith's painting of Ramsgate Sands in 1851, *Life at the Seaside*, and suggests that—transistor radios notwithstanding—our Victorian ancestors made far more noise than we do: 'Every seat is occupied; the boats and small yachts are filled; some of the children pour pebbles into the boats, some carefully throw them out; wooden spades are busy, sometimes they knock each other on the head with them, sometimes they empty pails of seawater on a sister's frock. There is a squealing, squalling, screaming, shouting, singing, bawling, howling, whistling, tin-trumpeting, and every luxury of noise. Two or three bands work away; niggers clatter their bones . . . The ginger-beer men and the newsboys cease not from troubling. Such a volume of uproar, such a complex organ of discord—I mean a whole organful—cannot be found anywhere else on the face of the earth in so comparatively small a space.'

The shock of all this, as we have seen, was too much for the Queen, but the fashionable world was less squeamish and Brighton gained fresh lustre in 1848 when, not for the first or last time, distinguished refugees chose to live there. Among those cast up on the south coast by the wave of revolutions in that year was the Austrian statesman, Prince Metternich, who—for his manipulations at the Congress of Vienna—had once been called the 'Master of Europe'.

Now, from September 1848 to April 1849, he lived quietly at No. 42 Brunswick Terrace, from whose windows 'the immensity of the sea charms the eye', as he wrote in his diary.*

Mémoires, Documents et Écrits Divers laissés par le Prince de Metternich, Vol VIII, (Paris, 1884)

On 17 November he added: 'I know no healthier place than Brighton. The air is pure, the temperature is extraordinarily mild and I know of no spot in the northern latitudes which unites so favourably those conditions of existence that one finds in the Midi. You only have to look at the vegetation to be confirmed in this opinion. In a garden a few steps from my house there is a magnificent tree, a *magnolia grandiflora*, quite as fine as the one that grew in the grounds of my villa on Lake Como in 1838; perhaps even more flourishing. Anywhere where the plants of the Midi do well in the open air is a good place to live. If, on top of that, the country is quiet and peaceful, then all the better!'

For most of Victoria's reign this golden, tranquil Brighton persisted for the visitor who had money and the leisure in which to spend it.

But there was another side to Brighton, which Dr William Kebbell, physician to the Brighton Dispensary, revealed in his *Popular Lectures on the Prevailing Diseases of Towns*, published in the same year that Prince Metternich was writing his eulogy.

'Our first-rate streets', he wrote, 'are not surpassed, if equalled, in cleanliness and general appearance by any in the world. The streets and districts of the poor, both in filth and general untidiness, and the squalor of the inhabitants, are a disgrace to any civilised people'; of the area around Edward Street he alleged that 'no one accustomed to fresh air can walk through these streets, especially in hot and moist weather, without being completely nauseated by smells.'

A similar picture is painted in the *Reminiscences* (1906) of Nathaniel Paine Blaker, who became house surgeon to the Brighton and Hove Dispensary in 1860: 'Opening into North Road, then called North Lane, between Bread Street and Gardner Street, on the site now occupied by Tichbourne Street, were two rows of buildings called Pimlico and Pym's Gardens. They were mere huts with a few feet of garden in front and were in a most dilapidated condition.

'The inhabitants, mostly fishermen, were of the lowest type, the families lived all crowded together, and I have seen on Sunday mornings girls of ten or twelve years old, or even a year or two older, walking in front of the houses absolutely naked. In the gardens and paths in front of the houses heads, skins and intestines of fish were lying about in every state of decomposition. Nothing could be worse than the sanitary conditions and yet there was a remarkable freedom from illness; though Bread Street above and Gardner Street below had their full share.

'I could only account for this by supposing that, being fishermen, they could get fish and so were well-fed; secondly, that the houses were so old and dilapidated that in spite of overcrowding plenty of fresh air got through the cracks and crevices and, lastly, that being very low (only the ground floor), there was plenty of sunlight and nothing to prevent free circulation of air.'

At certain times and places these two worlds would touch. The area Blaker describes was hardly more than a hundred yards from the Theatre Royal and a contemporary writer gives us a Daumier-like impression of the scene outside the theatre and in its adjoining streets in the '60's, after an evening performance of *Lady Audley's Secret* or *The School for Scandal*.

The author, whom we know only as 'a Graduate of the University of London', produced a most extraordinary guide-book to Brighton. Publications of this kind are usually designed to attract custom to the place portrayed, but this must have shocked and terrified its more timid readers. Any respectable tradesman, newly arrived in Brighton with his wife and daughters, and consulting this work to find out the best place for hearing a German band or the nigger minstrels, would surely have hustled his brood on to the next train back to London.

Published in 1860, it was called: *Brighton As It Is: Its Pleasures Practices and Pastimes—with a Short Account of the Social and Inner Life of its Inhabitants, being a Complete Guide Book for Residents and Visitors.*

'The object of this work is twofold', the preface explained. 'It is intended to serve both the purposes of a Guide Book and a Handbook of Social Science. To the Visitor it will afford all the Local Information necessary for his guidance, while to the Resident it will be a Work of Reference in regard to many interesting matters connected with the Moral and Social Condition of the Town, which have not yet been presented to the Inhabitants of Brighton in a collected and comprehensive form.'

Was he a sincere reformist or one of those tongue-in-cheek 'crusaders' who still help to sell newspapers? After asserting that 'one of the most efficient cures for social evils is publicity', he goes on: 'There is the Theatre in the New Road, conducted as theatres usually are, and attended with all those evils which experience has proved to be incidental to amusements of this kind. Close by there is a gin-palace with the usual appendages of plate-glass and flaring gas-lights, where prostitutes resort, in order to ply their sinful calling when the Theatre dismisses. The colonnade, after 11 o'clock, presents a very animated appearance, being then used principally as a promenade by the "women of the town", who are either there for the

purpose of entrapping the unwary or of keeping some previous appoint-
ment. The women for the most part observe the outward rules of propri-
ety, although, on some occasions, we have witnessed scenes of drunken
lewdness.'

Just around the corner from the theatre is Church Street which in 1860,
according to our author, was 'a locality not by any means remarkable for
its respectability'.

'Go along there any night', he wrote, 'and you will see hideous old
women, drunken old men, young men, and sometimes mere boys, hope-
lessly intoxicated, reeling and staggering in the road. There is also of
course the usual amount of cursing and blaspheming, which is sometimes
followed by an occasional fight, which terminates in the ordinary manner,
with broken heads and black eyes.'

Such scenes were commonplace in Victorian towns and particularly in
those that were undergoing rapid expansion as Brighton necessarily was.
A building boom was inevitable to cater for the massive influx of visitors
and new inhabitants. When the Graduate wrote his guide-book there
were over 13,000 houses in Brighton compared with 8,000 in 1841, the
year the railway came.

And the well-to-do visitor saw only what he wanted to see. The Rev.
Edward Bradley, who, as 'Cuthbert Bede', wrote *The Adventures of Verdant
Green*, a comic novel about undergraduate life at Oxford, was also the
author of a book about Brighton, *Mattins and Muttons* (1866), in which he
says: 'England can show no other spot where a continuous line of white
houses, the greater number of which are of palatial appearance and
dimensions, stretches for three miles along the sea-cliffs, and is backed up
by a mass of streets and squares forming a town large enough for the habi-
tation and requirements of more than 80,000 residents and more than
100,000 visitors. Brighton, in fact, is ten or twenty watering places rolled
into one . . . so much larger, grander and gayer than all the sea-bathing
resorts in England as to well deserve the title of their queen.'

Most of this building—still mainly in the 'Regency' style up to about
1860—had taken and was taking place on the hill-slopes near the station
and in the empty spaces between Brighton and Kemp Town (in the east)
and Brighton and Hove (in the west). Hove's expansion was, relatively
speaking, even more startling than Brighton's. In 1821 it had about 300
residents; by 1861, over 9,000.

Within living memory it was fashionable to sneer at Victorian buildings
and such enthusiastic defenders of their virtue as Sir John Betjeman, but

as contemporary architecture has become increasingly uninventive and arid (for which the architects blame their clients and vice versa) the self-confident structures of the latter half of the nineteenth century have been aesthetically rehabilitated and even the most eccentric of them gratefully accepted for their entertainment value.

Hotels and churches are among the most noticeable monuments of the Victorian era in Brighton.

The two hotels most likely to catch a visitor's eye are the Grand, with its white, Monte Carlo look, and the red-brick Metropole, both on the sea-front, between West Street and the West Pier. The Grand was, when built in 1864, one of the first hotels in Britain to be provided with an 'ascending omnibus' (i.e. a lift) and—with its 150 bedrooms— was the largest hotel in town. The Metropole was of somewhat later vintage (1890) and is visibly related to the Natural History Museum in South Kensington (they had the same architect, Alfred Waterhouse).

But it was also a great period for church building. Despite the godlessness described in *Brighton As It is*, this was not a town in which God was disregarded. The author tells us that in 1851, a year in which the town had a population of 65,500, a total of 18,500 people attended the Sabbath morning services of the Church of England, Independents, Particular Baptists, Society of Friends, Unitarians, Wesleyan Methodists, Primitive Methodists, Bible Christians, Lady Huntingdon's Congregation, the Isolated Congregation, Roman Catholics, the Catholic and Apostolic Church, the Latter Day Saints and the Jews.

An Anglican Church that is notable for its imaginative siting—on an island site to the north of the Steine—and as an early example of Victorian Gothic is St Peter's, built in 1824–28 and the Parish Church of Brighton since 1873. It was designed by Sir Charles Barry, then a young man, who, towards the end of his life, was to be the architect of the Houses of Parliament.

Later in the century there was to be the astonishing phenomenon of a family of church-building parsons—the Wagners. The Rev. Henry Michell Wagner was vicar of St Nicholas', a living which his grandfather had held before him. His father had not been in holy orders but had made a fortune as a hatter, money which his descendants were to disburse in the service of the Church. First, H. M. Wagner built St Paul's Church, West Street, in 1848 at his own expense of £14,000. Then his son, Arthur Douglas Wagner, vicar of St Paul's went on to build four more—St Mary and St Mary Magdalene in Bread Street; the Annunciation in Washington

Street; St Martin's in Lewes Road; and—the most famous of them and in its day the most controversial—St Bartholomew's in Ann Street. Towering above every other building in its neighbourhood, it is four feet higher than Westminster Abbey. As Nikolaus Pevsner says in his *Sussex*, it is of plain brick throughout and of 'no historical or local class', yet he describes it as 'an unforgettable experience'. He goes on: 'As far as East Sussex is concerned, it may well be the most moving of all churches . . . this tremendous church owes its existence to an individual's munificence and devotion.'

But in a lay context the most significant monument of all is, of course, the railway station. The front of what was originally an attractive Italianate building has been spoiled by later accretions and the whole is now threatened with 'redevelopment' (fiercely resisted by a 'Save Brighton Station' group) but it is still a continuing influence on Brighton's life.

Even though the majority of week-end visitors now come nose-to-tail along the London Road in their hot tin boxes, fine weather still brings trainloads of Londoners swarming down with all the enthusiasm of the 1840's.

The railway has also been responsible for the appearance of a theatrical 'colony' in Brighton. The fact that it is possible to catch the 'Equity Express' after a West End curtain and still reach home and bed at a reasonable hour has commended Brighton to Lord Olivier, Dame Flora Robson and many other well-known stage people.

But, most of all, it is responsible for the continuance of the strange race of commuters. They existed even in the days of the stage-coach, for William Cobbett wrote in 1823 of stock-jobbers who 'skip backward and forward on the coaches and actually carry on stock-jobbing in Change Alley though they reside in Brighton'.

A large number of Brighton's working population still earn their living in the City or Whitehall and spend two hours or more of five days in every week in—usually non-stop—trains.

They have many ways of adapting to this daily interregnum between two existences. Many sleep, becoming unconscious within seconds of finding a seat and—from long habit—waking automatically thirty seconds before the terminus. There is an intermediate group who doze fitfully over newspapers. Some beaver at office files. Some insulate themselves from all human contact in a book; others have even *written* novels and plays on the train. Some play bridge with fanatical intensity (these are among the more savage defenders of 'their seats' which—although no system of official reservation is operated—are denied to innocent non-commuters by a variety of stratagems).

The strangest commuting manifestation of all is the railway 'card'. There are small groups who invariably consort together for conversation and each group contains one member who is the accepted butt or wag. He (for it is always a man) usually gives the impression that his performance—for such it is—is the high point of his day, permitting a flowering of personality that is denied to him elsewhere. He expands visibly as he bustles on to the train and deflates as he passes through the ticket-barrier at the other end.

Perhaps a social scientist at the University of Sussex should write a doctoral thesis on commuters before escalating rail fares make the breed extinct.

CHAPTER NINE

Edwardian Interlude

'Edwardian England is a time and a land seen across the vast dark chasm of war. Over there the afternoons seem to linger in the mellow sunlight, the nights are immediately romantic. There is illusion here, of course, but it is not all a cheat: something *did* go, something *was* lost.'

J. B. Priestley: *The Edwardians* (1970)

The term 'Victorian' can have little meaning other than 'England between the years 1837 and 1901' because, socially, ideologically and in every other way, it was a period that covered so many 'Englands'.

'Edwardian England', on the other hand, is a term of far nicer definition—but by no means confined to the nine years that Edward VII was on the throne. It was a new era in which extremes were less marked—but class still 'mattered'; in which old standards of belief and conduct persisted—but no one took them quite so seriously. The common-sense, easygoing attitude which the stout gentleman with the pointed beard symbolised was the prevailing tenor of the nation long before the old Queen died, certainly by her Diamond Jubilee in 1897, probably ten years earlier.

Anyone wishing to experience something of the authentic 'feel' of this period cannot do better than to read two books which, taken together, give an almost three-dimensional sense of what life was like, in the 1890's, in Rottingdean—then an isolated seaside village, now a part of Brighton but, thanks to the cliffs, the Downs and its village green, still maintaining a separateness of character (it was the first place in the borough to form a conservation society).

Both books give us recollections of Sussex village life seen through the eyes of a child; that is, with a freshness of vision not yet dimmed by any cloudbank of experience. And there is much to be learnt from their juxtaposition because each child was standing on a different rung of the social ladder.

The first is *Three Houses** by Angela Thirkell the novelist, which includes a description of summers spent at Rottingdean in the house of her grandparents, Sir Edward Burne-Jones, the Pre-Raphaelite painter, and Lady Burne-Jones, who was Rudyard Kipling's aunt. (Their handsome, rambling old house, overlooking the green, bears a commemorative plaque.)

The other book is *A Song for Every Season—A Hundred Years of a Sussex Farming Family*,** in which the author, Bob Copper, gives an account of the village at the same period, based on the boyhood recollections of his father, James Dale Copper.

Jim, son of a farm waggoner, was born in a two-up two-down flint cottage in 1882, but there had been Coppers in Rottingdean certainly from the end of the sixteenth century and perhaps longer.

Miss Thirkell begins the Rottingdean section of her book with a charming description of what the journey from Brighton Station was like for an excited child perched on top of a horse-bus.

'It must have been a relic of early omnibus days in London', she writes, 'with seats beside the driver and a knifeboard on the top where one sat back to back, just like Leech drawings in old copies of "Punch".'

The preferred bus was that from the White Horse inn in Rottingdean. Appropriately drawn by two white horses ('so stout and competent'), it was greatly superior in the little girl's opinion to the competing vehicle from the Royal Oak.

'It came right up the steep hill into the station yard and was waiting for us at the end of the journey. We would willingly have clambered up to the seats beside the driver but they were usually reserved for lucky grown-ups and the most we could expect was occasionally to be jammed in, between a grown-up passenger and the driver, and allowed to hold the end of the reins when he gathered them up. Our Nanny had strong objections to our going outside, which were partly in the general scheme of repression and partly, I must now admit, a not unnatural avoidance of the responsibility of a child with quicksilver in its legs and sea-air in its brain being on the roof. So as a rule we had to ride inside with Nanny and the baby, though even here were compensations, for the bus actually had a door that was shut in cold weather and straw on the floor in winter, so that it was difficult not to find romance . . .

'By now perhaps I had been lucky enough to be perched up in front

---

*Oxford University Press, 1953   **Heinemann, 1971

between the driver and some friendly grown-up, with a broad leather strap across us both, much needed when the driver turned the horses' heads, and we drove down the long steep hill from the station, the bus almost pressing the horses' hindquarters. The driver held them well up, bracing his feet against the board in front, and we held on to the seat and were thankful for the strap which kept us from slithering down, especially when our legs were too short to reach the floor. Our bus had special privileges and was allowed to go along the sea front while other and inferior buses had to come and go by back streets. So we swung round to the right in Castle Square, leaving the Pavilion behind us, and there in front was the sea which we hadn't seen since Christmas, the pier, and the bathing machines hauled up from the tide. Past terraces and squares of Regency houses we clattered, delightful houses with great bulging windows overlooking the sea, some curved, some angular. Past the mysterious terrace of houses which were all black and were built, so Nanny used to tell us, of very hard coal, because the man who built them had made a fortune in it.' (Nanny was misleading her charges. Royal Crescent was built by a West Indian speculator, J. B. Otto, and the blocks of 'coal' were the mathematical tiles already noticed at Patcham Place.)

Leaving Brighton behind them they clip-clopped along the road at the top of the cliffs until the black sails of the Rottingdean windmill told them they were near their journey's end and prepared them for the last hill that plunged down into the village: 'Then the drag was put on, leaving those shiny smooth marks on the surface of the road, and we skidded down hill into the village while Charlie the conductor blew his long coaching-horn . . . The *White Horse* was the official terminus of the omnibus, but after delivering some parcels it would go round the village putting passengers down at their doors . . . Charlie blew his horn and we turned the corner, leaving the sea behind us, and drove up the village street. One needed eyes on both sides of one's head to see all the friendly shops and houses and faces that we passed . . . Stenning the baker whose buns perfumed the air, Mrs Mockford at the little fruit and chocolate shop which always smelt of ripe pears, Mr and Mrs Champion in the Post Office where you also bought spades and buckets, Read's Stores with the red-headed assistant. A glimpse up the hill on to the downs and we had reached the turning that went up past the forge to the Vicarage and then came to the butcher's house and and shop standing a little back from the road where Mr Hilder home-killed South Down mutton twice a week—meat of such juicy close-grained excellence that my brother was moved to describe the Sunday joint with tears in his eyes as "sainted mutton" . . . finally North End House and our grandmother's face at the window.'

It is clear from what one reads that both Angela Thirkell and Jim Copper were happy intelligent children, but it is equally apparent that each lived in a separate world, never touching more than the fringe of the other's and apathetic—or even antipathetic—to the possibility of penetrating any deeper

On occasion, in her reminiscences, Miss Thirkell herself draws our attention to this. This was not a High Tory household—Lady Burne-Jones would invite labourers and artisans into her drawing room and preach William Morris Socialism at them—but the children were indelibly caste-conscious. Angela's brother, after being hugged by the motherly cook, ran upstairs yelling, 'I don't *want* to be kissed by person in kitchen'; and she adds her own confession: 'This piece of snobbishness was only surpassed by my horrid self when, at a tea-party for village children, being told to hand round cakes, I said in a fat sulky voice, "I'm not a servant", which so horrified my grandmother that she was unequal to any kind of blame.'

But even she has her blind spots, as shown by this little sample of a typically Brahmin point of view: 'Another of our forbidden pleasures was to walk up and down this path from the front gate to the fence . . . kicking and shuffling the shingle with our feet. Some of it went into our sand-shoes and was very uncomfortable; the rest was left in untidy heaps till Ernest, the garden boy, came and raked it smooth again.' Again, she says 'there were two boys' schools in the village', by which she means private schools; the village school to which Jim Copper went did not register.

It comes vividly to life in his son's book. It was a Church of England School of five classes under the headmastership of a Mr Lloyd and the tuition fee was a penny a week. By the author's account there must have been times when it resembled Dotheboys Hall: 'The school curriculum was not confined to academic studies. No doubt Mr Lloyd reasoned that as these boys were the sons of working men and destined in the fullness of time to become working men themselves, some form of practical tuition should be offered them. The bigger boys could weed the garden, clean the windows or scrub out the school lavatories and in return they would receive at the end of the week a suitable number of mauve heart-shaped cachous.' If they transgressed 'Bandy' Lloyd would pummel them in the ribs with his fists or, in more extreme cases, cane them. One occasion for the major form of punishment would have shocked Lady Burne-Jones.

'Youngsters were still brought up on strict lines of discipline and if respect for elders and betters was not always earned it was rigidly enforced. Jim and his contemporaries, being members of the cottage community, had to pay suitable salutation to the gentry who lived in the large properties round the village green. The parson, the doctor, the land-owners and farmers all received due acknowledgement in the form of a doffed cap or a small bobbing curtsey from the girls . . . There was no resentment on the part of anyone, at least within our circle, at this order of things. It was accepted as the natural pattern of life; after all you sang about it in church on Sunday:

> *The rich man in his castle, the poor man at his gate,*
> *God made them high or lowly, and ordered their estate.*

'The penalty for not practising this code was well-known to all and the offence dealt with summarily. "Come out here, Jim Copper", the offender would be summoned before the headmaster. "You passed Parson Thomas on Pump Green yesterday afternoon and you didn't raise your cap" . . . the lesson that incivility to dignitaries would not be tolerated was driven home by Bandy's cane and carried back to Jim's desk in two stinging palms.'

For little Angela, Rottingdean was a holiday world where, at Christmas time, the Burne-Joneses would cheerfully give the boy carol-singers two shillings to get rid of them. For Jim it was a scrimping and saving work-aday world, which allowed him a halfpenny a week pocket-money; in which his mother and sisters were 'busy with their needles, turning shirt tails into shirts fronts'; and he held a tallow candle to give more light to his father as he mended all the family's boots on a winter's evening.

For holidays Rottingdean was, to use an appropriately period adjec-tive, a 'jolly' place. It had always prided itself on its differences from Brighton; never sought to imitate it. In Brighton Public Library there is a manuscript diary, dated 1814 and entitled *A Summer at Rottingdean*, whose anonymous author says proudly: 'The Company is always select—there being no Theatre or Gaming House to attract the dissolute and idle to throw away their time and fortune, nor will the common sort of vulgar gentility find here those attractions which Margate the Delightful Mar-gate offers, more pleasing to them as more nearly resembling their own habitations of St Mary Axe and Bucclersbury. Still this place will always have charms for the lovers of Quiet and Retirement who wish to enjoy the sea air—either for their Health or Pleasure uncontaminated by the Smoke and Noxious Air of More Crowded Watering Places.'

He is one of the few writers who have set down in writing what it was like to be inside a bathing machine as it bumbled down the beach: 'Here also is Bathing to Perfection where Gentlemen and Ladies turn out of their beds in easy negligence almost without their clothes and are slowly dragged in a Machine (which by its cracking seems about to drop you into the fluid beneath) by two old Matrons into about two feet depth of water. But here let me caution my male readers not to stay too long while bathing for if you do your persons and machines will be assaulted with a volley of flints and stones from the impatient and irritated ladies.'

By coincidence Miss Thirkell gives us a child's eye glimpse of the return journey (but some 80 years later, when the techniques were more sophisticated): 'Far above us on the cliff was a capstan from which long wire ropes, over which everybody tripped, hung down to the beach. A hook at the end of this rope was attached to the bathing machine and a donkey began to walk round and round the capstan hauling us up. It was a delirious joy to feel the little house beginning to move, to hear first the swish of the waves against the side and then the scrunch of the wheels in shingle as the donkey pursued his round and we went higher and higher up the beach.'

Since the middle of the century the camera had been adding its quota to evidences of the Brighton scene and we can therefore see for ourselves a vehicle known as a Daddy-Long-Legs which Miss Thirkell describes as a 'most preposterous machine'.

This—known officially as The Brighton and Rottingdean Seashore Railway—was the brainchild of a pioneer inventor of electrical devices, Magnus Volk, born in Brighton but the son of an immigrant German clock-maker. In 1881 he devised a street fire-alarm system; in 1883 he installed electric light in the Royal Pavilion; and in August of the same year opened Britain's first electric railway, a ten-seater car on a two-foot-wide track that ran for a quarter of a mile along the sea-front from the Aquarium to the Chain Pier. A year later he doubled the length of track by extending it to the Banjo Groyne and in 1896 he opened a further extension of three miles to Rottingdean, but this section was on an entirely new principle.

The track was *under water* and the double-decker 150-passenger car was mounted on iron stilts, 24 feet high, so that it rode clear of the sea whatever the state of the tide.

With an almost audible sigh for opportunities lost Miss Thirkell says: 'We were never allowed to go on it, partly because no grown-up thought it amusing enough to go with us and partly because it had a habit of sticking somewhere opposite the ventilating shaft of the Brighton main sewer and not being moved till nightfall.'

She also says this of the *Daddy-Long-Legs*: 'It was more like a vision of the Martians than anything you ought to see in a peaceful seaside village.' Did similar thoughts occur to H. G. Wells? There is a strong family resemblance to this freakish apparatus in those great iron octopi in which the invading Martians of *The War of the Worlds* strode across the Thames. His story appeared as a serial in *Pearson's Magazine* the year after the line opened and we know from his autobiography that this was the period when he and his wife 'began to wander about the south of England' on 'a tandem bicycle of a peculiar shape'.

Young Angela may have been denied a voyage on the sea-train with its red ensign, but she had rarer pleasures which many would envy her. Rudyard Kipling, who lived in Rottingdean at this time, was her 'Cousin Ruddy' and she describes how, on a hot August afternoon, she would 'lie panting on the shady side of a haystack up on the downs, a field of ripe corn rippled by the warm wind before us, with scarlet poppies and blue cornflowers gleaming among the wheat, and hear his enchanting voice going on and on till it was all mixed up in a child's mind with the droning of a threshing machine up at Height Barn . . .'

It was here that Kipling wrote the *Just So Stories* and he read them aloud to her: 'The *Just So Stories* are a poor thing in print compared with the fun of hearing them told in Cousin Ruddy's deep unhesitating voice. There was a ritual about them, each phrase having its special intonation which had to be exactly the same each time and without which the stories are dried husks. There was an inimitable cadence, an emphasis of certain phrases, a kind of intoning here and there which made his telling unforgettable.' (I quarrel with the 'dried husk' assertion; when I read the book as a small boy that 'inimitable cadence' came to me quite clearly from the printed page.)

It is a pity that the social taboos of the time prevented this impressionable child from investigating the world of Jim Copper which held joys that, though of a different texture, could be equally intense.

Having left school, he was a waggoner's boy, working with four heavy Shire horses—Tommy, Tipler, Prince and Swallow. A frequent job was to take a wagon of straw and corn the four miles into Brighton and bring back a load of dung—which the streets and stables of such a busy town could provide in prodigious quantities.

In later years Jim often described such an occasion to his son and this is how it appears in *A Song for Every Season*: 'The Brighton waggon was Jim's favourite job; he enjoyed the sense of occasion and the feeling of importance that attached to it . . . Jim's proudest moments were in Brighton town itself—striding down North Street at the head of the leading trace-horse, a brass-ringed whip over his shoulder, his head held high. The harness jingled and the sets of bells in the hames sent peals of music rattling through the streets, making the townsfolk stand and stare and the town dogs bark like fury. That was a proud moment for any boy.'

*　　*　　*

We learn something about what the town was like in the 1890's from *Brighton As I Have Known It*, a book by the popular and prolific journalist, George Augustus Sala, who was for many years on the *Daily Telegraph*. He had spent some of his childhood in Brighton and at the end of his life lived there again at No. 2 Eastern Terrace on the East Cliff. This book was his last (published in 1895, the year he died) and one suspects he occasionally looks at the contemporary scene through slightly rosy spectacles.

He recalls that there had been a general consensus of opinion that Brighton was ruined 'when Royalty finally abandoned the town' but in fact, he says, there was not 'any great falling off in the number of aristocratic and wealthy families who were permanent residents at the west and east ends of the town.' He approved of the frequent holiday excursion trains ('eminently conducive to an improvement in the physical and moral condition of the people') because they were good for trade while they did not 'in any way interfere with the comfort of more patrician visitors or of the residents'.

The fashionable season in 1895, he tells us, began in the first week in October and ended just after Christmas, a timing made possible by the fact that there were 'more days at Brighton when we can keep the windows open than in any other English town whatsoever'.

'So while people are shivering in London or groaning under the infliction of fog, the ladies are disporting themselves in open carriages in Brighton. In the morning the Front presents the agreeable spectacle of troops of ladies on horseback; some are independent Amazons and need no guidance, while others are under the care of skilful riding-masters;

children on ponies likewise abound . . . Between 3 and 5 p.m., the Front through King's Road to Kemp Town and on the Marine Parade is crowded with barouches, landaus, broughams, mail-phaetons and dog-carts and it must be a very inclement October and November at Brighton if the majority of the landaus and barouches are not open'.

The fashionable visitors left after Christmas, returned for a brief season around Easter-time and then deserted the town again before the arrival of that 'very deserving class of British people', the summer visitors.

But they were not the end of the story. Sala goes on: 'Ere the summer comes to a close fortunate Brighton is blessed with two more seasons. In July the more affluent members of the Hebrew community come down in large numbers. In August and September there is the tradesmen's season, which is also a capital one for the lodging- and boarding-houses. Thus, with the exception of the months of January and February, Brighton may be said to have a constant succession of remunerative seasons.'

Sala makes what I believe to be the first mention of American visitors to Brighton. He tells us that the Metropole hotel had introduced the novelty of after-dinner concerts 'in the spacious vestibule', at which smoking was permitted.

'These diversions are intensely appreciated by American visitors . . . their approval of these most humanising attractions is sufficiently shown by the alacrity they display in patronising hotels in London, Brighton and Paris where music, accompanied by cigars or cigarettes, forms part of the evening programme.'

But for the ordinary English holiday-maker with limited funds the basic pattern of activity (except for the innovation of the goat-chaise—now, alas, to be seen only in Brighton Museum) had changed very little since the beginning of the railway era, although it was perhaps a little less rumbustious by 1895 than in Richard Jefferies' day: 'Summer at Brighton means bathing; it means donkey-riding and driving in goat-chaises; it means the building of sham fortifications in sand or with pebbles on the beach; it means the collection of sea-weed and shells by the small folk; it means much reading by young ladies of cheap novels, or knitting, or in some way whiling away the time in shady places or on the Pier.'

The pier to which Sala refers must be the West Pier, opened in 1866 (whose preservation or demolition is a subject of acrimonious debate in present-day Brighton). Although the Chain Pier was not to be destroyed by a violent storm until the following year (1896), it was already considered unsafe and the Palace Pier, on which work began in 1891, was not to be completed until 1899, owing to recurring financial problems.

It will be recalled that although Sala made enthusiastic mention of 'wealthy families . . . at the west and east ends of the town' he carefully avoided any reference to the town-centre which, it would appear from other sources, had begun to have a neglectèd and depressing look at the time his book was published. The Pavilion, which now belonged to the Corporation, was so dilapidated that even the Prince of Wales was moved to comment on its being 'somewhat worn and faded' when he visited it in 1896; work on the Palace Pier went on by fits and starts behind a dismal hoarding facing the Steyne; and some of the adjoining hotels had fallen on hard times.

An hotelier, a close-knit clan of Jewish bankers and Edward, Prince of Wales, himself were all to play their part in generating new prosperity.

The first of these was the dynamic Harry Preston. He had run an hotel at Bournemouth since his early 20's and went to Brighton in 1901 when he was 42, a time of life when a man has either to make his mark or resign himself to the ruck. By all reports he was a born innkeeper, with an easy smile, a sharp eye and a card-index memory for potentially profitable names and faces. He particularly cultivated people in the worlds of the theatre and sport (including the new enthusiasts for motoring and aviation), in fact anyone whose publicity might cast some reflected limelight on his hotel business.

'My switch-over from Bournemouth was not a run from depression to prosperity', he tells us in his *Memories*,* 'but rather the reverse. Brighton had been Queen of the South, but she was suffering from a wave of depression . . .

'The Royal York** which I was taking over was derelict. I had to rebuild it from top to bottom, and sink in it every penny I possessed, and a good deal I did not possess. Across the way, on the island site opposite the Palace Pier, was the Royal Albion, which eventually I acquired . . . those were great days. We put our backs into it and soon brightened things up and got some names that meant something in the guest book.' One of the names was that of Arnold Bennett, whose inclusion of the York in *Clayhanger* as the 'Royal Sussex' did business no harm.

In 1906 when he was beginning to make headway he was infuriated by an article in the *Daily Mail* in which Brighton as a holiday resort was 'attacked, hit over the head, shoved into a coffin and buried' (his words).

---

*Constable, 1928   **Now municipal offices

He stormed into Carmelite Street and with his usual flair persuaded the editor to publish his own, opposite view.

But in fact the *Mail* was expressing what was, at that time, a commonly held view. Lewis Melville, who wrote a number of popular books on the town, was gloomily nostalgic in *Brighton: Its History, Its Follies and Its Fashions* (1909): 'Cheap excursions for "trippers" and half-guinea Pullman trains for the well-to-do have changed the character of the place out of all recognition . . . Brighton is interesting only in its past. As Bath has become the home of the half-pay officer, so Brighton has developed into the Cockney's Paradise, the Mecca of the stockbroker and the chorus-girl. The glory indeed has departed. The Pavilion stands, an object of derision; the Steine is still open to the public, but it is encircled by a network of tramways; while the houses that look on this erstwhile favourite spot, once occupied by aristocratic visitors and residents, have been converted into cheap boarding-houses. The town now boasts mammoth hotels and theatres and music-halls in all parts and you may now obtain everything but quiet.'

Even at this early date the author brought the motor-car under attack as a threat to amenity. He grumbled at the altered aspect of the promenade, 'once an agreeable lounge, but now made hideous by the hooting and whirl of the motors that have taken the place of the well-appointed, splendidly-horsed barouches and four-in-hands'.

But even as he wrote these words new life was being breathed into Brighton's reputation by Edward VII, son of the woman who had done her best to deflate it. He had stayed at the Pavilion as a child and had sometimes come to the town for opening ceremonies and the like during his long wait for the throne; but it was after his accession in 1901 that he began to make more frequent visits. For the second time in its history Brighton was to profit from its popularity with a prince who liked good living and pretty women. In February 1908 he stayed for a week with his daughter, the Duchess of Fife, who had a house at No. 1 Lewes Crescent, Kemp Town. 'The King is declared to be deriving both health and enjoyment from his holiday', recorded the *Brighton Herald*, 'and this fact and the fact that he has been rejoicing in floods of sunshine is being chronicled in the press all the country over. Nothing could exert a finer influence on the fortunes of Brighton. Nothing could be more calculated to bring about an influx of rank and fashion to the town.'

One reason for Edward liking Brighton was his friendship with the Sassoon family, whose conversation entertained him and whose hospitality was lavish. They were the descendants of Sheikh Sason ben Saleh, who had been the head of the Jewish community in Baghdad in the latter part of the eighteenth century and the beginning of the nineteenth. Since the 7th century a Jewish trading community had flourished in the city, as in other parts of the Islamic Empire, but as the Ottoman power declined conditions became less settled and local Pashas began to persecute the richer Jews for their private profit. The old sheikh sent his son David to re-establish the family under a newer and, as it appeared, more stable regime—that of the British in India.

Under a close family caucus the Sassoons' business interests spread rapidly in India and the Treaty Ports of China until, in 1858, it became necessary to establish a London office, a task entrusted to David's son— Sassoon David Sassoon. He died in 1867 but his younger brother Reuben succeeded him and in 1876 was joined by another and elder brother, Abdullah, soon to be known as Sir Albert Sassoon.

Through the Rothschilds they were introduced to London society and the Prince of Wales; for their services to the Raj they were even looked kindly upon by the newly crowned Empress.

Sir Albert bought a rambling house at No. 1 Eastern Terrace, and two of his brothers were installed in attractive villas at Hove—Reuben at 7 Queen's Gardens and Arthur at 8 King's Gardens. Other members of the clan joined them and the allegation by Henry du Pré Labouchere, the editor of *Truth*, that Brighton was a 'sea-coast town, three miles long and three yards broad, with a Sassoon at each end and one in the middle' soon became an understatement in more ways than the obvious one.

Apparently King Edward most enjoyed staying with the Arthur Sassoons. 'There was nothing royal in these visits', says Cecil Roth in *The Sassoon Dynasty*,* 'which did a great deal to bring down the monarchy to the eye level of the man on the Brighton promenade, who was after all the man-in-the-street on holiday . . . The King would go out each day for his stroll along the lawns or on the front, arm-in-arm with his host; and the aroma of his cigar would be snuffed up by his admiring subjects. Cake-shops in the town would proudly display letters of commendation from Mrs Sassoon, indicating how his Majesty had enjoyed their products . . .'

There are still signs to be found of this attractive, exotic family who adapted so elegantly to their new environment. At the north-east corner of Paston Place Sir Albert built himself a mausoleum which, harking back to

*R. Hale, 1941

his origins in Baghdad and Bombay, looks like a miniature Pavilion. He was buried there in 1896 and his son, Sir Edward, in 1912, but their remains were removed by the family in 1933. For a time it was used as a store by a firm of decorators; now it houses a discothèque—the 'Bombay Bar'.

Less noticed, because its reddish tinge blends with the brick pillar into which it is set, is a granite panel recording a benefaction by the widow of the first of the English Sassoons and grandmother of Siegfried, the author.

The plaque is at the western entrance of a little public park in Hove called St Ann's Well Gardens (a chalybeate spa in Regency days and still earlier a copse where Downland shepherds watered their flocks). It reads:

THE PLOTS OF LAND

COMPRISING THE

TWO CROQUET LAWNS

WITH FRONTAGES NORTH &

SOUTH OF THIS ENTRANCE

WERE PRESENTED TO

THE BOROUGH OF HOVE

BY

MRS FLORA SASSOON

AND OPENED TO THE PUBLIC

1ST MAY 1913

ALD. BARNETT MARKS, J.P.

MAYOR

It is an oddly prosaic memorial to Fahra Reuben who, as a petite quick-tempered girl of 14, was married in Baghdad to the 18-year-old Sassoon David Sassoon and ended her life in a British seaside town where she was remembered as an elegant little old lady who asked questions in a strange sing-song voice and rarely listened to the answers.

*　　*　　*

There is still one place in Brighton where it is possible to breathe a little of that calm Edwardian air—at least as it would have been enjoyed by a family that had position and money, tradition and taste.

Preston Manor, which lies north of central Brighton, on the London Road and adjoining Preston Park, is a Georgian house, built on the site of a mediaeval manor. It came into the possession of a William Stanford in 1794. That the public can now see it—much as it was when the family lived there—is attributable to one of the countless tragedies of the 1914–18 war. The last of the Stanfords, Vere Benett-Stanford, was an artillery major who contracted a disease of the chest through giving his respirator to his sergeant during a gas-attack on the Western Front. He died of it in 1922 and Sir Charles Thomas-Stanford (the historian of the Civil War in Sussex) who had inherited the manor in the early 1900's decided to bequeath it to the town of which he had been Mayor and which he had represented in Parliament.

CHAPTER TEN

World War One
to World War Two

'Long anticipated by a few, and persistently scouted by many, the great conflagration of Europe has broken out . . . Much has been heard of late of our national decadence . . . The time has come for the test. Every Englishman and woman must do their duty.'

Brighton Gazette, 5 August 1914

Newspapers are a particularly useful source of material for the historian. Like diaries (unless subsequently tampered with) they have the merit of letting us know what was being written 'at the time'. Memoirs, auto-biographies, histories can be touched up in the light of after-knowledge, but a newspaper tells us what the editor or the reporter (or the person reported) was thinking on the date printed at the head of the page. That is to say, it is what the journalist was thinking if he felt strongly enough about an issue to decide that he should and could guide the minds of his readers; if he was not of this persuasion (and in this he would belong to the majority) he would at least be putting into words his intelligent guess at what most of his readers were thinking that day and would like to have mirrored back to them.

The files of the *Brighton Gazette* are interesting for this reason. Although Guy du Maurier's play about a German invasion, *An Englishman's Home*, had been staged in the West End five years before and 'Saki' (still famous for his short stories) had written a novel on the same subject, *When William Came*, (William being the Kaiser), there would seem to have been small conviction among the general public that war of any kind—let alone the mindless slaughter of the trenches—was impending. In 1939 even the most blinkered sections of the population had been jolted into a real-isation of what the inevitable sequel of Munich was to be, but in 1914 euphoria—in Brighton, at least—seems to have been total.

The *Gazette* of 1st July had this opening paragraph to *Topics of the Day*, a column of editorial comment: 'Assuredly the summer season has opened auspiciously at Brighton. The visitors who have started the vacation early have caught some of the good things. June was as sunny a month as May and April were brilliant, and 1914 already has to its credit more sunshine than any of the past seven years at the completion of the first six months.' An 'increase of revenue from chairs on the sea-front' (i.e. deck-chairs hired to holiday-makers) is the subject of gratified reference and then there comes this idyllic passage: 'To crown a splendid June, the First Battle Squadron arrived off the town between one and two o'clock yesterday afternoon, under conditions which can only be described as perfect. The radiance of the scintillating sea, the vibrant atmosphere seemed to rob the leviathan warships of their grim and sinister associations . . . the jolly tars are sure of a welcome when they land to-day.'

What may have been some first flickerings of doubt appeared three days later, when the editor wrote (whether ironically or optimistically is not clear): 'Old prints of Brighton give a view of the town on the occasion of one of the ancient bombardments by the French. Such a thing is unthinkable in these days, when everybody is talking of peace and at the same time arming to the teeth.'

In succeeding issues the news stories given the most space were the execution of a murderer at Lewes Gaol and the trial of a coloured man accused of killing his wife, but finally on 29 July the truth began to seep through: 'It must be something very special to impress the people gathered at the seaside, seeking impressions if possible, far removed from the problems and perplexities of life. But we had only to visit Brunswick Lawns, the piers, the promenades, or the churches on Sunday to feel there was an atmosphere of tension and anxiety everywhere . . . People were pre-occupied with events on the other side of the Channel . . .'

The same issue gave some comfort to its more apprehensive readers by re-printing the judgement of *The London Magazine* that 'the German infantryman is too fat . . . lacks the dash of the French, the doggedness of the Russian, the fatalism of the Turk, or the practical adaptability of his British rival'.

On 1 August the editor was no doubt speaking for many when he expressed his incredulity that a large-scale war could really happen: 'If the worst comes to the worst it will be a nice commentary on the much-vaunted civilisation, humanitarianism and brotherhood of nations. The Balkan States cutting each others' throats is not astonishing to anyone

who understands the races in that part of the Continent but the two Triple
Alliances, banded together for Peace and Defence, starting a wholesale
European War, suggests the last word in cynicism.'

Then, knowing his readers, he struck a more business-like note: 'There
was considerable speculation as to the effect of the war on the holiday season at home. The general impression was that unless this country is
entangled in the quarrel the restriction of Continental travelling should
increase the rush to the English pleasure resorts . . .'

By the time the next issue of the *Gazette* appeared, on 5 August, the war
and Britain's involvement in it were facts and the paper took the firm pat-
riotic note quoted at the head of this chapter. It also told its readers that
on Bank Holiday Monday (the day before we declared war) 'the weather
could not have been better', that there were large numbers of summer visitors and that 20 excursion trains arrived before noon.

A reporter noted that—to remove possible doubts as to their
nationality—an Italian ice-cream 'Jack' and a Dutch oyster-merchant
had decorated their sea-front stalls with Union Jacks. But at this stage of
the war there seems to have been no great animosity towards the Germans. One paragraph noted: 'A large number of Germans have had to
give up appointments in the district and return to their military duties and
many of these made some genuine friendships which were interrupted
with genuine regret.'

A curious incident occurred at the end of that month, on Sunday 30
August. Presumably because of censorship delays it was not reported in
the *Gazette* until 9 September, and—again no doubt for censorship
reasons—no explanation of the incident was published subsequently.
This was how it read:

AN OBJECT LESSON

'One of the most instructive object-lessons of the war yet witnessed on
this side of the Channel was brought under the notice of the crowds on
Brighton front on Sunday week. From out of the dense sea mist that
hung over the water, there appeared a large hydroplane. Beyond the
whirr of the engine there had been nothing to indicate its approach. It
dropped on to the water a few yards from the shore and quietly glided
on to the sands, where the aviator and his companion landed. A Union
Jack fluttered from one of the uprights, and everybody imagined it was
one of our aerial fleet. Judge then of the surprise when it transpired that
it was a French machine that had travelled across the Channel and

landed without a challenge. It was all right under the circumstances, but many people asked what was there to prevent a German seaplane carrying a Union Jack as a blind, doing the same thing? And if one could do it, why not twenty?'

In fact it was to be more than a quarter of a century before there were air attacks on Brighton, but the realities of war showed themselves in the *Gazette* before the end of the year when columns were given over to 'letters from the Front' and the steadily lengthening casualty lists. But, oddly to our eyes, the paper still found room for the equally long lists of 'Hotel and Boarding House Visitors' newly arrived in town, a surviving echo of the Master of Ceremonies of Regency days.

By the following year the *Gazette* was remarking that Brighton 'had an important role to play in providing a haven of refuge' and that the parade on the sea-front 'recalled the palmiest days of October and November thirty years ago'. From 1916 onwards their numbers were augmented by Londoners seeking to escape the bombing raids by Zeppelin airships.

Not that Brighton, any more than any other place in Britain, could be completely insulated from the slaughter. The rumble of guns could be heard from across the Channel and the telegraph boy became a dreaded figure as more and more husbands and sons died in the Flanders mud. There were also constant reminders in the blue uniforms and red ties of the maimed men who had survived. Many of these were the turbaned soldiers of the Indian Army for whose wounded the Pavilion and the Dome had been transformed into a hospital of so appropriate a form that one suspects some Whitehall warrior had a moment of whimsey (although the suggestion is officially ascribed to King George V).*

From time to time Brighton schoolchildren were taken to visit the hospital and one of them published his recollections** which throw a strange little spotlight on the scene and the time: 'All around the Pavilion were ornamental iron railings (now gone) and fixed to these was a closely boarded wooden fence about 8 feet high (for privacy), to stop the general public from peering in. As some of the Indian soldiers got better of their wounds (a good many had arms and legs amputated) they wanted a little more freedom and so it became a familiar sight to see a crutch flung over

---

*On the Downs, a mile north of Patcham, there is a monument to those who died, the *Chattri*. It is on the site of the burning *ghat*.
**Albert Paul: *Poverty—Hardship but Happiness* (Queen Spark Books, Brighton, 1975)

the high fence and then another crutch, followed by an Indian soldier with one leg scrambling down the high fence.'

Less welcome (except to the tradesmen) were the munitions profiteers who—with fat cigars and gold watch chains as badges of their new wealth—were pilloried in *Punch* of those years. No doubt their ostentatious good living helped to feed the indignation of the poorer inhabitants of Brighton whose wartime deprivations led to their making a protest march in 1918 to the offices of the Brighton Food Committee, carrying banners saying: 'The Wives and Children of our Fighters shall not want for Food'.

An event which was at least to end the butchery of the trenches whatever other problems it left unanswered took place quite close to Brighton, at the country house of Danny, which we have already noticed in the chapter on the Civil War. Visitors are still shown the table round which the members of the Imperial War Cabinet—including Lloyd George and Winston Churchill—sat on 13 October 1918, to consider the terms which President Wilson had suggested for an armistice with Germany. It was there that the cable was drafted and signed authorising him to proceed with the negotiations that eventually silenced the guns.

The Kaiser's war was followed by a slump as the Napoleonic Wars had been and on both occasions the subsequent discontent among working men gave rise to similar hallucinations of impending revolution, exacerbated in the 1920's by the Communists' seizure of power in Russia. Something of this hysteria came to the surface in Brighton during the General Strike of 1926. There can hardly have been a more moderate document than the T.U.C. memorandum of 1 May which called the strike, with its insistence that 'a strong warning must be issued to all localities that any person found inciting the workers to attack property or inciting the workers to riot must be dealt with immediately'.

But a week later the *British Gazette*, the official news-sheet produced by Churchill at the Stationery Office to fill the vacuum left by the many newspapers which had ceased publication was alleging 'an organised attempt . . . to starve the people and wreck the State'; promised that the number of special constables would be raised to 50,000; and notified all ranks of the armed forces that 'any action which they may find it necessary to take in an honest endeavour to aid the Civil Power will receive, both now and afterwards, the full support of His Majesty's Government'. In the same number of the *Gazette* Lord Grey of Fallodon said: 'The issue now is not what the wages of miners should be, but whether democratic

Parliamentary Government is to be overthrown. . . . The alternatives are Fascism or Communism.'

A special 'strike issue' of the *Brighton and Hove Herald* on Saturday 8 May said the strike had 'descended . . . suddenly but relentlessly' on the two towns on the preceding Tuesday. The residents had awoken to find themselves in 'a strange perplexing world' without trains, trams, buses or newspapers. (One result of the strike, according to the *Herald*, was a rush to buy 'wireless installations'; to a TV-nourished generation it is mildly surprising to read: 'Many residents who had not previously dreamt of adding wireless to the amenities of their lives, have this week become the proud possessors of sets'.)

On 7 May an incident occurred which, in the light of the subsequent treatment of demonstrating strikers by the police and magistrates, does much to illuminate contemporary attitudes.

On that day a procession of 200 strikers was marching down East Street towards the sea, carefully avoiding any collision with a cordon of police that had been thrown round the Town Hall. The *Herald* describes what followed:

'Just as the strikers passed the constables a two-seater car driven by a woman approached from the sea. Seeing the strikers the woman must have stamped on her accelerator. At a bound the car leaped forward at tremendous speed. It literally ploughed its way through the body of the strikers. Several were flung to the ground. The others had to leap for their lives, right and left. Instantly there was furious turmoil. Men recovered from the shock dashed for the car, and some of them mounted the footboard. The police drew their truncheons and flung themselves on these men. In the fierce confusion it was impossible to say whether any actual blows were struck. The constables dragged a man off the car. the woman continued to drive on at speed and turned swiftly up North Street. Who she is no one could say. She came within an ace of causing bloodshed.'

It would be surprising if, despite the confusion, no one had the presence of mind to take the number of her car. Yet there is no hint, then or later, that any attempt was made to bring the woman to court.

A quite different attitude was taken by officialdom towards those accused of violence in what the *Herald* headline was to call 'The Battle of Lewes Road'.

A key element in the strikers' strategy (throughout the country) was to bring public transport to a halt and a popular form of retaliation by their opponents was to act as volunteer train-, bus-, and tram-drivers. On 11

May a crowd of strikers, sympathisers and mere inquisitive onlookers gathered outside the Brighton tramways depot in Lewes Road, under the impression that an attempt was to be made to bring the trams back into service. Actually, plans had not progressed this far. What was being attempted was the introduction of volunteer drivers and conductors *into* the depot so that they could be trained in their duties. When these arrived, under police escort, the crowd refused to move and a number of arrests were made before the 'blacklegs' (or 'volunteers', according to the sympathies of the observer) could be hustled into the depot.

The Chief Constable, Charles Griffin, then ordered the road to be cleared, a task entrusted to 300 foot police and 50 mounted specials, advancing in wedge formation, who forced the strikers back until they reached the Saunders Recreation Ground.

These 'mounted specials', who figured prominently in what followed (to be subsequently lauded by one side and vilified by the other), were an auxiliary body which the Chief Constable had raised for the period of the strike and placed under the command of 70-year-old retired cavalry officer. During their short period of existence they acquired several nicknames: Griffin's Uhlans; Harry Tate's Own (after a well-known music-hall comedian); the Black and Tans (there were some former members of the Royal Irish Constabulary among them); and Preston's Horse. This last cognomen was given because one of their number was Harry Preston, the hotelier, now 68 years old (he tells us in his *Memoirs* that his equipment included a knuckle-duster).

The *Herald* obviously approved of this group, 'well set-up on their fine horses, determined, formidable'. carrying 'ugly-looking shillelaghs with knobbed ends'.

At this point in the proceedings some hooligan in the crowd threw a bottle at a constable and this was followed by stones and bricks. This is how the *Herald* described the sequel:

'The Saunders Recreation Ground salient continued to be a thorn in the side of the constabulary's successful battle . . . so orders were given to the mounted auxiliaries to relieve the situation. They could not enter the playing field from the Lewes Road and the only alternative was to charge through the crowd in Hollingdean Road and gain admittance by the side entrance. This manoeuvre created panic among the onlookers who were scattered in several directions. Many people narrowly avoided being knocked down by the horses. The mounted auxiliaries were flourishing their clubs and one man in the crowd was seen by a journalist to receive a sharp blow on the head. But for the main part the riders were trying not to strike and such blows as were dealt seemed to be unintentional.'

The report added: 'The flying stones, the panic rush, the thud of blows, the shrieks of frightened women and children, caught in the confusion invariably aroused by violence—these things did not belong in civilised Brighton.'

By the standards of civil disturbance in some other countries it was a mild and bloodless 'battle'. Eye-witness accounts collected by an author avowedly sympathetic to the strikers* speak of bruised backs and nervous upsets (particularly among children) but nothing more sensational. On the other side, the subsequent court proceedings mentioned only one constable injured in the mouth by a stone, a mounted special hit on the back of the head by a brick and several horses struck by stones. (The *Herald* reported that one constable 'had his trousers badly torn'.)

In view of this the sentences imposed by the magistrates seem unduly harsh. Twenty-two men appeared before an emergency magistrates' court the same evening charged with incitement to riot and assaults on the police. They were remanded in custody until the next morning when—despite a spirited defence by A. J. Grinstead, a Labour Councillor—17 of them received sentences of hard labour of from one to six months; three others were fined; a youth (said to be mentally abnormal) was bound over in the custody of his father; and another youth was remanded in custody for eight days.

The General Strike was already over when the men were sentenced. During the lunch adjournment the news was broadcast that the General Council of the T.U.C. had called it off. Grinstead asked the Bench (consisting of the Mayor and several ex-Mayors) to adjourn the case and postpone sentence, pleading that 'if there is peace, it should be a general peace', but the Mayor referred darkly to 'mob law' and would not be moved. 'All have cause for thankfulness', said the *Gazette* approvingly, 'that the menace of the general strike is over, and over, too, not by surrender to the forces of disorder and tyranny, but by the victory of the British commonsense over Moscow-inspired illusion.'

Violence of a different kind, springing not from want and indignation

*Ernie Trory: *Brighton and the General Strike* (Crabtree Press, 1975)

but from professional viciousness, had often been associated with the Brighton racecourse. The author of *Brighton As It Is* in 1860 had found Brighton's crime-rate very moderate considering the 'size and fluctuating nature of the population', but deplored the serious offences that were committed by 'strangers from London and elsewhere, and particularly at the time of the races, when criminals of all classes flock to the town'. And Sala commented in 1895 that 'although a great deal of money is taken by the tradespeople during the racing season, Brighton is not very sorry when that season comes to an end. What may be called the camp-followers of the noble army of sportsmen are not the most agreeable of mankind and it is only during the "Sussex Fortnight" that the law-abiding Brighton people sedulously lock their front doors.'

Such troubles reached their peak in the 1930's when this and other racecourses were infested by gangs who offered 'protection' to book-makers and took their vengeance with razors on those who refused to be blackmailed.

Scotland Yard's Flying Squad, with the aid of Detective-Sergeant Collier, of Brighton C.I.D., who knew most of the wanted men by sight, broke up the last of these gangs ('the Hoxton Mob') at Lewes racecourse in June 1936. But the sense of menace these yahoos could generate has survived in Graham Greene's *Brighton Rock*: 'Hale knew they meant to murder him before he had been in Brighton three hours . . . '.

However much racecourse bullies and other deviants may have caught the public eye it was a man of quite a different stamp who was the really significant figure of Brighton in the inter-war years; significant because it was his far-sighted views and his determination in implementing them that preserved a wide-sweeping arc of downland on Brighton's borders. Ahead of his time he appreciated two things: that a community must have visible, recognisable boundaries if it is to *be* a community; and that town-dwellers need the refreshment of green walks and wide vistas if they are not to degenerate into petulant automata.

This man was Herbert Carden. Nowadays many of the most devoted defenders of Brighton's amenities are comparative newcomers to the town, but there have been Cardens in Brighton since the seventeenth century, if not earlier. At St Nicholas' Church there used to be (until it disappeared in the Victorian 'restorations') a stone of 1699 to the memory of Abigail, wife of Nicholas Carden, to whom an obviously devoted son (or daughter?) had inscribed the following lines:

> '*O dear Mother, you*
> *Are gone before*
> *And I a wratch*
> *Waite at the door*'.

Another ancestor (of whom he was particularly proud) avoided a food riot in 1756 by selling corn to the poor of the town at a reduced price; and Samuel Carden, of the fishing boat *Robert and Mary*, was among those whose death during a storm in Seaford Bay in 1856 was recorded on a monument erected by public subscription in the Extra-Mural Cemetery.

He must have been given an early interest in local government by his father, John Carden, who was for 30 years Clerk to the School Board and its successor body, the Education Committee. Educated at Brighton Grammar School, Herbert was admitted as a solicitor in 1889. Six years later, when he was only 28, he was elected to Brighton Council and was for a time a member of Hove Council as well! At first some of his more conventional colleagues disparaged him as 'a young man in a hurry', but he made his mark so forcibly that he became an Alderman after a phenomenally short initiation of eight years.

The rapid rise was all the more remarkable in that he was a professed Socialist at a time when anyone so labelled was liable to be regarded at best as socially unacceptable and at worst as an anarchist. Seated among colleagues to whom the idea of 'municipal trading was anathema' he nevertheless by his own brand of personal magnetism hypnotised them into becoming pioneers in several forms of civic enterprise: a Corporation telephone system; Corporation electricity; Corporation trams; Corporation acquisition of property for road-widening; Corporation housing estates handsome enough to earn international as well as national esteem; Corporation purchases of downland to give Brighton its 'green belt'.

It was, on the face of it, ridiculous that Carden, a total abstainer, a non-smoker, and energetic sea-bather, a devotee of 'physical jerks' and the 'simple life', should be attacked by opponents as an 'apostle of optimistic extravagance', but exactly the same words could well have been used by his admirers to describe the dash with which he risked his own money to save open downland which would otherwise have been corroded by bricks and mortar.

His technique was to buy on his own account and then hope to resell to the Corporation at the same price, thus avoiding the escalation that would have occurred if it had been known that a public body was in the market for land. It was in this way that he secured the Devil's Dyke and similar areas for public use. He claimed that between 1896 and 1936 Brighton was able to buy over 12,000 acres at a cost of only £800,000.

When he was made a Freeman of the Borough in 1926 (four years before his knighthood) he was able to say: 'Take a little walk in imagination . . . We have walked the whole of the way from the parish of Rottingdean right round Brighton up to the Dyke Road *on our own ground*. Future generations will say we have done something which I don't believe has been equalled in any other town in the country.'

On his death in 1941 journalists were to describe him as 'The Father of Modern Brighton' and one who 'had loved Brighton, served Brighton and preached the gospel of Brighton to the exclusion of any other interest in his restless, strenuous life', but the best vignette of this unusual man was given by Sir Charles Thomas-Stanford many years before in an interview with the *Sussex Daily News*: 'I regard Alderman Carden as a most useful motive force; and his alarum prevents the town from going to sleep. He reminds me of those gas-engines which transmit power by means of a series of small explosions. The machinery of government and the inertia of ordinary man supply the regulating control. But his engaging personality, his unfailing good humour, his almost boyish enthusiasm, and his breezy certitude as regards results are very stimulating. Even where he is most in error the by-products of his enthusiasm may be valuable.'

His death in 1941 could be said to have come too early or too late. He was by then aware of the dangers with which the Hitler war threatened the town, but did not live to see that—by the standards of the time—Brighton was to come through comparatively unscathed.

It was not until the war was over that most of the inhabitants were to realise just how serious that threat had been. The people of Brighton, like everyone else in Britain, their minds conditioned by memories of Guernica and the film of H. G. Wells's *Shape of Things to Come*, expected high explosive and poison gas to rain down on the populations of all the belligerent nations within minutes of the declaration of war. When none of this happened that comatose interlude the journalists called 'the phoney war' set in. It was like an afternoon tea-party at which everyone pretended that the ticking of a time-bomb was only the familiar sound of the old marble clock on the mantelpiece.

Brighton and Hove were as crowded with holiday-makers as usual and the first intimation that their war was not to continue on these happy-go-lucky lines came on 10 May 1940, when a badly shot-up seaplane made a forced landing off Brighton beach. A bather waded out to help the pas-sengers ashore. They were the Foreign Minister of Holland (with his wife) and the Colonial Minister. The Blitzkrieg had begun. Holland was com-pletely overrun by 15 May and Belgium surrendered on the 25th. Next day the British Army, cut off from its allies and from any line of retreat by land, began to escape by sea from the port that had figured in British (and Brighton's) history so often before: Dunkirk.

In a memorandum to the Luftwaffe that day, Admiral Schniewind said: 'Evacuation of troops without their equipment is conceivable . . . if large numbers of smaller vessels, coastal and ferry steamers, fishing trawlers, drifters and other small craft are used . . .'.* His opponents came to the same conclusion and by the end of the evacuation on 4 June more than 335,000 troops had been saved. Many Brighton craft ferried back and forth and many were sunk by dive-bombers: the pleasure paddle-steamers, *Brighton Queen* and *Brighton Belle*, two of Brighton's like-a-nice-trip-sir? *Skylarks* and fishing boats with such unwarlike names as *Our Doris*.

France asked for an armistice on the 17th and Winston Churchill told the Commons on the following day: 'What General Weygand called the Battle of France is over. I expect the Battle of Britain is about to begin. Upon this battle depends the survival of Christian civilisation . . . The whole fury and might of the enemy must soon be turned against us. Hitler knows he will have to break us in this island or lose the war . . .'

If everything had gone according to the German plan much of that 'fury and might' would have been concentrated on Brighton in September 1940.

Initially Hitler shared Admiral Raeder's view that Britain could be made to sue for peace by air attacks and a naval blockade alone, but by 2 July he had decided that 'a landing in England is possible, providing that air superiority can be attained and certain other necessary conditions ful-filled . . .' and a fortnight later issued an invasion directive under the code-name, *Operation Sea Lion*.

On 15 August the Fuehrer decided that preparations should be made with a view to the first landings taking place on 15 September, and a clarifying directive stated: 'Main crossing to be on a narrow front; simul-taneous landing of four to five thousand troops at Brighton by motor-boats and the same number of airborne troops at Deal–Ramsgate. In

---

*This and other quotations from German documents are taken from *Hitler and His Admirals* by Anthony Martienssen (Secker and Warburg, 1948)

addition on D-1 day, the Luftwaffe is to make a strong attack on London, which would cause the population to flee from the city and block the roads.'

By 27 August the plan was that the landings should be in four main areas: from Selsey Bill to Brighton; from Beachy Head to Bexhill; from Cliffs' End to Dungeness; and from Dungeness to Folkestone. The first operational objective was that the Army should establish a line from Southampton to the mouth of the Thames.

Shipping for the invasion began to move to embarkation ports on 1 September; D-Day was still to be 15 September. Two days later it was decided to postpone embarkation until the 20th. On the 14th the Fuehrer ordered a further postponement because the Luftwaffe had not established the necessary degree of air superiority. On the 17th his War Diary records that the enemy Air Force was 'by no means defeated' and he postponed *Sea Lion* indefinitely. It was not finally cancelled until January 1942.

Anyone who has had first-hand experience of a beach-head can visualise the devastation that would have overtaken Brighton had those landings planned for September 1940 taken place.

Some measures of defence were taken when France fell—the beaches mined, the sea-front barricaded with sandbags and barbed wire, gaps blown in the piers by Army sappers, a battery of naval guns and a number of machine-gun posts set up—but whether or not these could have prevented the enemy from establishing a foothold, there is no doubt that a collision between British troops in a do-or-die mood and the Wehrmacht with their tails well up after the successes of the Blitzkrieg would have reduced Brighton to a heap of smoking rubble.

The town had had its first air-raid in July and, on the afternoon of Saturday 14 September (the eve of the date originally fixed for *Sea Lion*), had one of its worst raids of the whole war, when 20 H.E. bombs were dropped on Kemp Town. Air attacks on the two towns were to continue for four years. Although they were mostly of the hit-and-run variety over 200 people were killed and nearly 1,000 injured. Over 280 houses in the two boroughs were destroyed, over 900 seriously damaged and 19,000 slightly damaged, but no building of historical interest suffered any serious harm, the narrowest escapes being the crashing of a German aircraft into St Nicholas' Churchyard and a bomb falling on the Pavilion lawns.

CHAPTER ELEVEN

What's Past and What's to Come

'. . . the element of personal taste enters into
everything, with its magnifying glass and
its automatic simplifier.'

James Thurber: *Alarms and Diversions* (1957)

In 1945 when, against all the probabilities, the buildings which constituted the architectural heritage of Brighton and Hove had emerged
almost unscathed from five years of enemy action, a proposal was made
which was to have far-reaching effects on the future of the two towns; but
not at all in the way which its originators intended. It was recommended
to Hove Town Council by its officials that two justifiably famous groupings of Regency houses (Brunswick Square and Terrace; and Adelaide
Crescent) should be demolished to make way for blocks of flats.

The shocked reaction of all people of discernment is preserved for us in
the archetypal conservationist invective which Antony Dale included in
his book, *Fashionable Brighton**: 'The suggestion was so astonishing as to be
almost incredible. But, still more amazingly, it was passed by the Council
for eventual execution. Naturally such a decision was greeted with almost
universal outcry, not only in Brighton and Hove, but throughout the
country, amongst all who have any knowlege or appreciation of art and
architecture. It is earnestly to be hoped that such ignorant destruction
will never take place. But if these noble groups of houses were so
demolished, the Corporation of Hove and their officials would thereby
acquire for themselves the doubly melancholy distinction of being the
most destructive municipal authority in the whole of England and also of
having reduced their own Borough to the position of having not one single
building of architectural merit in the town.'

---

*Oriel Press, 1967

From boyhood Antony Dale had himself lived in a Regency environment—at Kemp Town. His grandfather had bought No. 46 Sussex Square in 1902. Antony's mother inherited it and he lived there for 50 years. The Dales were the last people to occupy the whole of one of the Sussex Square houses as a family residence rather than as a series of one-floor flats. (In 1962 Antony Dale finally acquiesced in the passing of the *Upstairs, Downstairs* era—there were 108 stairs in No. 46—and moved to something more manageable under modern conditions.)

From Brighton College he went to Oriel College, Oxford. He trained as a solicitor but when, in implementation of the 1944 Act, the Ministry of Town and Country Planning set up an historical buildings section he was invited by its head, Sir Anthony Wagner (one of his contemporaries at Oriel), to join him as an investigator listing buildings of special architectural interest in Kent and Sussex.

He and D. L. Murray, the historical novelist, had tried to form a local civic society as far back as the 20's, but public opinion was not then ready for it. In 1939 they had plans to form a Brighton branch of the Georgian Society, but the war intervened. Finally, in December 1945, they found two like-minded enthusiasts who agreed that the time was ripe for going ahead. One was William Teeling, who had been elected M.P. for Brighton the preceding year, and the other Clifford Musgrave, Brighton's Director of Art Galleries and Museums (a post which he held for 30 years, for much of which he lived in the Royal Pavilion). This time their ideas rode to public favour on the wave of indignation set up by the Brunswick and Adelaide proposals and the Regency Society was formed at a public meeting in the Pavilion. (After publicity in the national press—including an article by D. L. Murray in *The Times*—no more was heard of the idea that Brunswick Terrace should be demolished.) A Regency Festival Exhibition in 1946 established the new organisation as a force to be reckoned with, as it still is. Antony Dale, secretary for many years, has as keen an eye as ever for the potential vandal and the Society's new president is that Laureate of denunciation, Sir John Betjeman.

The idea that a local authority should control new building if it threatens to harm the local amenities is not a twentieth-century invention. Included in the mandate of the Society of Twelve ('eight Fishermen and fower landsmen') set up to govern Brighton's affairs in Elizabeth I's reign was the following provision:

'If any man hathe heretofore builde erect or sett upp anye Wall pale shedd or any such like things whatsoever Or yf anye shall erecte builde or sett upp anye house wall shedd or other suche like thinge whatsoever to the annoyannce of the market place or of the Blockhouse there And shall not uppon warninge geven him by the Conestable or his deputye for the tyme beinge pull downe or remove awaye the same within tenn dayes after suche warninge given That then he shall forfeite 20s and be further punished by the discreson of comissioners.'

Again, an Act of Parliament in 1825 gave the Town Commissioners such powers that 'any noisome or offensive buildings which they may deem a nuisance in the town, they have power to remove, with or without compensation to the owners'.

To what extent our ancestors exercised these powers we do not know, but if and when they did it was almost certainly on grounds other than aesthetic. The Tudor provision was obviously designed to avoid any interference with the commercial transactions of the market or the effective defence of the town. Certainly at that time there was no intention to preserve antiquities; from Henry VIII's reign onwards, for example, the vacated monasteries were merely regarded as convenient stockpiles of ready-worked building material.

We should also be given pause by recognising that tastes in architecture change from century to century; often, nowadays, when television so drastically shortens the lifetime of novelty, from decade to decade. For instance, Brighton's pride and the conservationists' cardinal preoccupation is its Regency architecture. But listen to J. A. Erredge, whose *History of Brighthelmstone* appeared in 1862.

After rather grudging lip-service to the effect that the squares and crescents were 'magnificent' considering 'the general state and style of architecture' and 'the rapid rise and development of the town', he goes on to indicate his own enthusiasm for Victorian Gothic (patronising Sir Christopher Wren, *en passant*!):

'During the close of the last, and the beginning of this century, architecture had reached its lowest ebb in England. Our true indigenous Gothic had almost passed into a tradition: Classic models, from their extreme ill-adaptation to our climate, had undergone such deterioration, that the application of the term even to the best of later works was an absurdity. The influence of Sir Christopher Wren had been of the most baleful character; not that he himself was deficient in genius, but that his style, which hardly attains to grandeur even in the Metropolitan Cathedral, was of a character that inevitably deteriorated in feeble hands . . . there cannot fail to be regrets upon the Brighton it might have been. Supposing, for example, that an earlier recognition of the claims of Gothic and an English style had taken place. Suppose that the public buildings, instead of being of the packing case order in beauty—hollow cubes with a sham frontage of stuccoed pilasters—had presented the variety in structure and beauty in detail which is found in a minor degree in St Peter's Church.'

He confessed to wishing Brighton had retained its mediaeval or Tudor aspect, preferring houses 'with roofs like over-sized wigs' and 'hanging stories one projecting over the other' to 'the most elegant and super-naturally genteel of our modern terraces'.

Of course the best example of the weathercocking of public taste is the Pavilion. To begin with nearly everyone—except, presumably, the Prince Regent—disliked and ridiculed it.

Cobbett likened it to a box crowned with turnips and tulip bulbs; Sir Walter Scott thought it a great eyesore; and Mary Berry, Horace Walpole's friend, said in her journal for 1811 that it was 'more like a china-shop *baroquement* arranged than the abode of a Prince. All is gaudy without being gay; and all is crowded with ornaments without being magnificent'.

Nor, as we have seen, was the young Victoria enamoured of the Pavilion, preferring to make Osborne on the Isle of Wight her seaside retreat. By 1848 she had gutted the Pavilion, transferring all the furniture and fittings to her other palaces.

In 1849 a Bill was brought before the House of Commons which would authorise the relevant department of Government to 'sell or otherwise dispose of or *pull down*' the Pavilion, and in fact the firm of Cubitt were rumoured to have offered £100,000 for the property with the idea of demolishing it and putting up rows of houses on the site.

If to-day's conservationist campaigners think that hairbreadth escapes and the unpredictable gyrations and apathies of public opinion are modern phenomena they should study this case and take heart. A few days after the first reading of the Bill a town meeting decided to petition against the sale and in two days 7,406 signatures were collected. At the second reading the Bill was passed to a Select Committee who, hearing that a further town meeting had favoured the Pavilion being bought by the inhabitants of Brighton, gave the Town Commissioners a month in which to make a decision to purchase; failing such a decision within that period, the property would be offered elsewhere.

On this understanding the Town Commissioners withdrew their

opposition to the Bill which received the Royal Assent on 1 August. Whereupon a town's meeting agreed to buy the Pavilion for £53,000 (a bargain considering that the land and buildings had cost George IV seven times that amount). But at this late stage some of the townspeople began having second thoughts. The events then following are described by J. G. Bishop in *The Brighton Pavilion and its Royal Associations*, which was published in 1876:

'Notwithstanding the immense advantage it was likely to prove, and has proved, to the inhabitants, to have the Pavilion property in their own hands, there was strong opposition to purchasing it; and many stormy meetings were held in connection with the subject. But the opposition sprang chiefly from ill-feeling and jealousy entertained towards the Clerk to the Commissioners by members of that body, and by several leading Vestrymen of the time . . .'

Brighton did not become a Borough until 1854 and was governed (as it had been since 1773) by a body known as the Town Commissioners. In 1849 there were 112 of these, a third of whom were elected by public vote each year. The Clerk at this time was Lewis Slight, who had taken up this position after a successful career in the shoe-trade. Probably because of an independent attitude acquired as a man in private business he did not altogether fit into the accepted pattern of a tug-the-forelock public servant (fortunately as it happened) and was nicknamed 'The King of Brighton' by critics who alleged that he had the Commissioners under his thumb.

Bishop continues: '. . . in the early part of December, 1849, after all the preliminaries were settled, and the town was pledged to carry out the agreement to purchase, an attempt was made to re-open the whole question. A memorial, signed by 160 names, was presented to the Parish Officers, requesting them to rescind all former proceedings, but the Parish Officers declined to act. On the 20th of the same month, a Vestry meeting was held to receive the Draft Bill for the purchase; it being necessary to have a special Act of Parliament for this purpose. The approval of the Bill was moved, when an amendment was proposed, to the effect, that it was undesirable to proceed further in the matter . . .'

Then came Mr Slight's bombshell: '. . . a very long and heated discussion took place, to which Mr Slight added not a little by his having been to London on the previous day unknown to the Vestrymen on the Committee, and signed the contract for purchase.'

The infuriated oppositionists succeeded in forcing through a motion that the Bill and the whole question of purchase be dropped but, in spite of this—and one can see the hand of Slight here—a two-day poll was organised to test public opinion. By the end of the first day there were 555 votes against purchase and only 408 in favour, but at the final count the pro-Pavilion party scraped home with a majority of 1,343 votes to 1,307. (What, one wonders, had happened to the 7,406 signatories of the original petition?)

Although the sycophantic author of the 1828 edition of *Brighton As It Is* (published when there was still a faint hope of George IV being wooed back to Brighton) enthused over the way in which 'the brilliant taste and gifted imagination of his Royal Highness instantly seized the glowing images which the mind of the artist (Nash) originated and portrayed' in order to produce a 'a pile not more unique in appearance than graceful in execution and beautiful in effect', even guide-books could rarely find a good word for it. The 1900 edition of *Sussex* in the 'Little Guides' series called it 'architecturally contemptible' and Ward, Lock & Co's *Brighton and Hove* for 1911–12, describing the evolution of the building from 'a respectable farmhouse' to its present form said: 'Persons who complain of the appearance of the structure to-day should spend an hour or so looking over the prints of what it was! For downright ugliness the Pavilion of 1788, or even that of 1818, can hardly have had an equal.' Two years earlier Lewis Melville, a popular writer on Brighton and its history, had called it 'an object of derision' and 'a palace the tastelessness of which is so remarkable that the humourists of two centuries have sharpened their wits upon it.'

It is, then, less surprising than it appears at first sight, that Herbert Carden was no friend of the Pavilion. The conservationists of to-day have good cause to revere his memory for his preservation of the green hills around Brighton, but his views on architecture make their blood run cold. In 1913, after a tour of German spas which impressed him greatly, he proposed that the Pavilion be 'scrapped' and 'a palatial Kurhaus' be built in its stead.

By 1935 he had deleted this project from his visions of the future, perhaps because in that year a book appeared whose elegant advocacy was to make admiration of the Pavilion respectable: *Brighton* by Osbert Sitwell and Margaret Barton. The tone of the argument is in this passage, postulating the Prince of Wales's participation in the creation of the final structure: '. . . did there not, perhaps, linger somewhere in his memory, as he consulted and pored over the various plans, the music of those haunting lines, published not so many years before,

> *In Xanadu, did Kubla Khan*
> *A stately pleasure dome decree?*

And, in fact, the phrase "a stately pleasure dome" precisely decribes the effect of the Pavilion, which shares with the lines we have quoted an identical dream-like quality.'

But in 1935 Sir Herbert Carden (as he had by then become) advocated other changes in the town which the majority of modern opinion would find just as shocking as his earlier plans for the Pavilion. Yet they must have commended themselves to many Brighton and Hove residents of the time—and those not the least prosperous and influential—for they were proudly set forth in an article prominently displayed in a photogravure supplement which the *Brighton and Hove Herald* published to celebrate the Silver Jubilee of King George V and Queen Mary. It was entitled *The City Beautiful: A Vision of New Brighton.*

One proposal was to make a clean sweep of all the Regency buildings facing the sea, at least so far as the eastern end of Hove and the adjoining areas of Brighton front were concerned.

'In place of the gaunt, basemented houses, badly converted into so-called flats,' he wrote, 'stately new buildings to house the new residents must arise. Embassy Court—that modern block of flats designed by that talented young architect, Mr Wells Coates—has shown us the way to build for the new age. Along our water front new buildings such as this must come and with their building will disappear many of the mean buildings that lie behind the present front.' And a half-page 'artist's impression' of the New Brighton emphasised his intention.

Embassy Court stands cheek-by-jowl with Brunswick Terrace, to whose defence Antony Dale was to spring in 1945. Here is what he says of it in his erudite guide, *About Brighton**: 'The visitor will not fail to notice a vast block of flats named Embassy Court which adjoins the easternmost section of Brunswick Terrace and which is the last building on the Front within the Borough of Brighton. This has been more criticised than any other building in Brighton or Hove. No doubt if it stood elsewhere, it would be possible to allow that the flats had architectural merits for a building of that kind. But standing as they do immediately next to

---

*Published by the Regency Society of Brighton and Hove, 1976

Brunswick Terrace and towering above its carefully regulated proportions, they are a glaring example of architectural bad manners and worse
town planning.'

Sir Herbert also wanted to clear the maze of narrow streets that mark
the site of mediaeval Brighton—The Lanes: 'All the clutter of old buildings around Market Street should be swept away, making room for modern buildings . . .'

These were the sincere, disinterested views of a thoughtful man, proud
of the town in which his family had lived for 300 years or more and sol-
icitous for its future. It is interesting to set them against the results of
recent opinion surveys which were concerned with discovering the things
which attracted visitors to Brighton—and it is on its ability to attract visitors (of several varieties) that the prosperity of the community still
largely depends.

It was in 1972 that the Corporation decided to carry out a three-year
survey with the object of collecting reliable data on visitors and their
views, e.g. where they came from, why they came, how long they were
staying, how much they would spend, what they liked and disliked, etc.
Organised and supervised by Mr James S. Tems, Senior Lecturer in
Tourism at Brighton Technical College, it is probably the most comprehensive survey of visitor traffic to a British resort that has ever been
made. Visitors have been questioned three times a year (spring, summer,
winter), sometimes by Town Hall staff but mostly by students of the
Higher National Diploma Course in Hotel and Catering Administration,
which is run by the Department of Management and Business Studies at
Brighton Polytechnic and serviced by the Hotel and Catering Department of the Technical College.

The final analysis of the nine reports gathered over the three years has
not been completed but one constant factor has been the high rating visitors have given to: The Lanes; the Pavilion; the town's parks and gardens; and the surrounding countryside. (In addition to being ahead of his
time in his concern for the Downs, Sir Herbert Carden started removing
the prison-like railings from Brighton's parks as far back as 1923.)

The Lanes are now 'probably Brighton's top attraction', according to
the Tems report, and yet in 1833—as J. D. Parry tells us in his *Coast of
Sussex*—this was a despised plebeian quarter housing 'humble emporiums
of industry' and 'shops of every description, each endeavouring to attract
the passenger by the promise of cheapness', where on Saturday nights
could be seen 'the anxious wife of the artizan, diligently seeking to lay out

her small pittance . . . in the most advantageous manner'.

Even as late as 1895 George Augustus Sala was writing: 'There is another district of Brighton to which visitors from London rarely pay much attention and the very existence of which in many cases they altogether ignore—this is the lanes, a labyrinth of narrow alleys approached from North Street and where, mingled with shops of a very humble character, are a number of places for the sale of curiosities . . . bargains in the way of old porcelain, gilt bronzes of the First Empire, carvings, ivory statuets . . . The lanes are undoubtedly a very ancient part of Brighton, but their very existence is unknown to the great majority of visitors to the place.

'Some of these days, it may be, a reforming Corporation will arrive at the conclusion that these narrow and tortuous alleys are unworthy of the dignity of Brighton and they will swept away to make room for new and imposing streets.'

Another significant comment by Mr Tems is that 'it is noticeable that overseas visitors are more appreciative of Brighton's architectural styles than British visitors', significant because in the ten years since 1964 the percentage of visitors from overseas increased from 3 per cent to 22 per cent, The largest national contingent is from Germany (14%) but the U.S.A., France and Scandinavia come a close equal second (12% each). By continents the largest group, as might be expected, is from Europe (66%) followed by North America (18%), Asia (8%), Australasia and Africa (3% each), Central and South America (2%).

When asked their reason for coming to Brighton one of the most frequent answers from foreigners was: 'I am attending a language course'.

Brighton is one of the towns on the South Coast of England which have benefited from the fact that, since World War II, English has become the almost universal *lingua franca*. So much of the literature of science and technology is written in Britain and the areas it colonised (notably North America) that few people, wherever they are born, can go very far in education or business without it. It has become the short-cut of communication that is used not only in multi-lingual areas like the Indian sub-continent, Malaysia and much of Africa but in situations like that of a sheikh in Abu Dhabi who wishes, for example, to discuss a desalination scheme with a water engineer from Japan.

The need for a rapid growth in facilities for teaching English became apparent as soon as the Marshall Plan and the United Nations relief agencies began to palliate some of the distresses the war left behind, but it was not until the 50's that most countries eager to learn had the money to do anything about it. The first language-school centres were Oxford, Cambridge and London (these are still the largest), but soon similar establishments began to flourish in a number of holiday resorts on the south-east coast, popular because of its equable climate and its proximity to London.

Brighton is now third or fourth in the 'league' of provincial centres. The number of students of all kinds receiving all categories of instruction is not easily arrived at. The six schools in Brighton and Hove 'recognised as efficient by the Department of Education and Science' (and regularly inspected by that Department and the British Council)* are known to have between 6,000 and 7,000 students a year, but the total number—including those attending summer schools—must be at least five times greater.

Those who come to schools that provide tuition throughout the year usually do so either because they need the language in commerce or industry (many are trainees or executives sent at their company's expense) or wish to attain greater fluency in the language before going on to a British university or technical college. They come from over 40 countries in Europe, the Americas, the Middle East and Far East. Although the effervescent teenagers of the summer schools are most noticed in the town, the age of students taking longer-term courses ranges from 16 to 70 and the average is about 25.

Most of them live with local families while studying and the two towns are fortunate in having acquired—in the language schools and the University of Sussex—an antidote to that preponderance of old faces that can threaten any south coast resort civilised and salubrious enough to appeal to the elderly retired. Statistics published in the *East Sussex County Structure Plan 1975* reveal a continuing tendency in both towns—whose combined populations now total nearly a quarter of a million—to move away from that mingling of generations that is essential if any community is to retain its sense of proportion.

They show that from 1961 to 1971 the percentage of Brighton's population which was of retirement age r e from 21% to 23%; the comparable figures for Hove being 29% and 30%. Thus Hove's figure is a little above and Brighton's still a fair way below the county average of 28%. This itself is high compared with the 16% recorded for England and Wales and is

---

*These are members of ARELS—the Association of Recognised English Language Schools.

caused, so the report says, by the 'high level of immigration of persons in the 60–65 age groups'.

It is, therefore, providential that there are now three institutions of higher education with about 9,000 full-time students in the locality: Brighton Polytechnic, (including the Faculty of Educational Studies); Brighton Technical College; and the University of Sussex. All these have students not only from all parts of the United Kingdom but from many foreign countries as well. The proportion of the latter is over 25% at the Technical College (half of them from Malaysia) and 16% in the case of the University which, from the outset, has prided itself on its international interests and outlook.

The idea of a university in Brighton was first mooted in 1911. It was yet another of the shapes in Carden's crystal ball. He was chairman of the Education Committee at the time and wanted a university 'so that our boys could hold their own with the youth of Germany and the United States during the difficult 25 years ahead'. But it was not until 1960 that it began to be built (with Sir Basil Spence as architect) near the village of Falmer on a parkland site that was formerly part of the estate of the Earls of Chichester.

Of its 4,000 students 88% live either on campus or in Brighton and 53% of the 2,000 staff also live in Brighton. The university makes a studied attempt to cultivate good-neighbourly relations. A 'Town and Gown' Club provides a pleasantly convivial forum for the discussion of problems that concern either or both; and the Gardner Centre for plays, music and exhibitions is also popular common ground. The student group, 'Link-Up', helps to run an adventure playground, gives old people a hand with their housework and shopping, and provides a volunteer work-force at a local hospital.

The permanent staff have had a noticeable impact on organisations outside the university. Seven per cent of the academic faculty and six per cent of the non-academic faculty belong to civic societies and 14% and 12.9% respectively to cultural and educational societies. In both these areas the level of participation by the staff of Sussex is about twice the national average for universities.

There is little doubt that some of the impetus behind the proliferation and continued liveliness of conservation societies in Brighton has come from the staffs of these institutions of higher education—although those who are active in this field grumble that more of their colleagues do not follow suit. There are now about 20 such societies in the area: some like the

Regency Society, the Brighton Society and the Hove Civic Society are wide in their coverage both of subject-matter and ground; others like the Old Patcham Preservation Society or the Brunswick Square and Terrace Association are concerned only with a strictly defined area; and others again have a single subject like 'Save Brighton Station' or the 'We Want The West Pier' campaign.

Brighton provides a fertile soil for movements both of advocacy and protest. There are a number of reasons for this. First there is the academic infusion already noticed. Secondly a high proportion of the retired are still years away from geriatric inertia; in fact, many of them, missing the bustle of their business or profession, find compensation in the excitements of agitation. Thirdly, about five per cent of the working population commutes to London and is often in a good position to alert local organisations to new or impending ploys by government and commerce.

The motives for joining are various. Some find understandable enjoyment in twisting the tails of those set in authority over them. Some, having spent large sums on the 'gentrification' of the house in which they live, are opposed to any change in the urban environment which could threaten their investment. But the majority are people of a genuinely altruistic turn who do not spare themselves (or, on occasion, the feelings of their opponents) to fight for the causes in which they believe. As always, these organisations are kept in being by a few individuals willing to give time and expend nervous energy not only in the arena of debate but in the drudgery of paper-work.

Typical of these is Mrs Selma Montford, secretary of the Brighton Society. Arriving in England from the West Indies in 1939, she spent much of her childhood at Oxford and her interest in old buildings dates from that time. She came to Sussex in 1965, helped to form the (local) Preston Society in 1971 and the more widely motivated Brighton Society in 1973. She is a lecturer in fine arts at the Brighton Polytechnic and the mother of four children, but still manages to devote some of every evening to the work of the Society, putting in an average of ten hours a week. Whenever her indignation is aroused she launches a letter at the editors of the two local papers, the *Argus* and the *Gazette*, and in a good year has 25 of them published.

Two major controversies have agitated Brighton in recent times: one for the preservation of something old; the other for the prevention—or at least the substantial modification—of something new.

The new project is the Marina or yacht-harbour. The first of a number of schemes to provide Brighton with a harbour was propounded in 1806. Its progenitor, a civil engineer named Ralph Dodd, said Brighton was 'the largest place in Europe so near the seashore without a harbour or shelter for shipping' and proposed there should be two stone piers, one beginning at the bottom of West Street and the other at the bottom of East Street, extending nearly 800 feet out to sea and then curving inward to enclose an area of 14 acres, providing harbourage for 200 sailing ships.

His declared intention was to provide much-needed shelter for the fishermen 'without hindering the valetudinarians'. Despite the fact that the coal-brigs unloading directly on to the beach left a film of black gritty dust on the water that can have contributed little to the health and comfort of the 'valetudinarians', it was they (and the townspeople whose living depended on them) who won the day and defeated the project. 'The plan of the intended harbour has drawn crowds of people of all ranks and descriptions to the *Old Ship*', a local newspaper reported on 21 March 1806. '. . . The inhabitants of the place are at present in some little degree of commotion, in consequence of the bill brought forward by one of the county members, Mr Fuller, and passed once in the House of Commons, for a jutty or jutties to be erected on this part of the coast, and immediately in front of this town. The inhabitants here are generally of opinion that such a measure, if ever it were to be carried into effect, would prove very destructive to their interests, and, as such, they feel themselves perfectly justified in exerting their united efforts to prevent it.'

A second scheme was projected in 1809, again without success. In 1823, as we have seen, the Chain Pier was completed and 19 years later it was suggested that it could form the centrepiece of a mercantile harbour, being flanked on each side by a breakwater of cast-iron plates filled with concrete. This came to nothing as did a number of other nineteenth-century proposals, one of which would have linked the Chain Pier with the West Pier to form a yacht harbour.

George Augustus Sala advocated a similar project as a profitable investment in *Brighton As I Have Known It* in 1895—the year before a storm finally destroyed the Chain Pier: 'Although there is no shipping here, as there is at Hastings, the sea—what with fishing smacks and the sailing boats during the regatta season—is seldom without a sail. That which Brighton principally needs, from a nautical point of view, is a commodious yacht harbour, which, without much difficulty, could be constructed by means of groynes . . . It would bring large numbers of affluent yacht-owners to the town and vastly inceeearity as a pleasure resort.'

Sala's final sentence accurately states the purpose which the developers say they have in mind for the harbour whose breakwater was completed in April 1976 (although the associated residential and entertainment complex had still to be built).

The Marina, as it is fashionable to call it, was first thought of by a local garage owner and amateur yachtsman, Mr Henry Cohen, who presented a scheme to Brighton Council in 1963. Being at that time a little uncertain of their wisdom in having recently turned down proposals for a £400,000 municipal yacht-harbour of modest dimensions, the Council greeted the Cohen plan with enthusiasm and the planning committee gave its unanimous approval in the following year.

Then came the first crop of objections. Cohen wanted to build his 3,000-berth harbour—together with a heli-port, hovercraft base, swimming pool, hotel, 247 houses and flats—on the foreshore that lies immediately below the Georgian dignities of Kemp Town, a stronghold of the Regency Society. The Society and other objectors raised such a barrage of protest that the promoters soon decided to work on a site three-quarters of a mile further east. Another outcome of this initial skirmish was an agreement that none of the new buildings should rise above the cliff-top.

The original scheme was estimated to cost £9 million. A new version presented in 1965 contained a number of new features such as a 1,000-seat cinema, a night-club and a casino; the cost had risen—modestly by the soaring standards of the 70's—to £11 million.

'About £100 million' is the cost figure usually mentioned in public discussions and newspaper reports of the current scheme which the Minister of the Environment approved in May 1975 after two planning enquiries, two town meetings, two town polls, and debates in both Lords and Commons on two private Bills.

One continuing complaint is that provision originally made for a large dinghy park and beach has been dropped from the scheme since 1970 on the grounds (a) that boats navigating the harbour entrance needed power; and (b) they had to be provided with waste-retention systems to avoid pollution. At the second public enquiry in December 1974 Richard Reeve, a former Commodore of the Brighton Sailing Club, said '. . . the small boat owner (and by this I mean not only the dinghy owner but also the owners of small sailing and motor cruisers) is completely ignored'.

Sir John Betjeman objected on more general grounds. He did not appear at the enquiry but said this in a letter to a member of one of the protest groups, the Marina Action Committee: 'I cannot understand why those who defend this piece of developers' greed regard such an expansion of Brighton as inevitable. No one who has the good fortune to live in Brighton will think that a garish pleasure slum built on the water will benefit the town.'

As I have said, the result of this second enquiry was made known in May 1975 and, if the proof of impartiality is that neither side shall be completely satisfied or unbearably disappointed, then the Government inspector passed with flying colours. The developers wanted the number of berths limited to 2,000; he increased them to 2,061. They wanted 1,450 houses and flats; he limited the number to 850. He would not countenance their proposals for buildings that would have been 83 feet high; he ruled that none of them should exceed 49 feet, which is half cliff height. He also pleased many objectors by criticising the design of the residential buildings for being 'rigid' and 'uncompromising'. On the other hand, he sanctioned the developers' plans for a shopping, exhibition and entertainment complex, and for a 500-bedroom hotel with restaurants, swimming pool and health hydro.

The inspector described the Marina as 'a bold, imaginative and attractive scheme', adding: 'There is every reason to think that the ratepayers will gain financially from the successful completion and operation of the Marina, quite apart from the many less tangible benefits that will accrue to Brighton'.

Most local people hope that this sanguine forecast will be justified in the event but there is a lingering fear that financial backing from banking and insurance groups will run dry at some stage and realise what the *Brighton and Hove Gazette* has called 'the threat of a half-built harbour being left to scar the coastline'.

This anxiety was allayed for a time in April 1976, when the last caisson to complete the breakwaters was laid. Even those who share Sir John Betjeman's misgivings about the scheme as a whole can admire the gracefully curving structure that encloses 77 acres of sheltered water (compared with the modest 14 acres proposed by Dodd 170 years earlier). One hundred and ten caissons, each 38 feet high, 40 feet in diameter and 600 tons in weight had to be laid on the sea-bed by a 1,200-ton crane to create one of the largest marinas in the world.

But at the official ceremony held in May to mark this stage in the progress of the scheme Mr Richard Hodges told reporters that he was unable to say when the hotel and all the other ancillaries of the full £100 million plan would 'get off the ground'. And all the old doubts were aroused afresh when, only a fortnight later, he informed the Council that—although all the caissons were laid—he still had to raise £11½ million of the £40 million which would be the cost of the complete harbour structure. If he was attract the necessary capital, he claimed, he had to augment the anticipated income of the marina by charging an entrance fee to people who wished to walk along the harbour wall.

In a statement at a press conference he explained: 'It is important to remember that the company does not have access to or assistance from any public funds. It does not itself have the funds to complete the marina. It has to obtain the money from financial institutions, and in order to do so it has to demonstrate to them that there will be an adequate return'; and he added: 'Without these charges the completion of the marina could be a problem.' The Council agreed reluctantly to his application—but only on condition that local residents were allowed free entry.

The enthusiasm of the Brighton Corporation for the Marina—at least in its earlier rhapsodical phase—invited comparison with their apparent apathy towards a coincidental issue which has aroused even higher feelings in the town: whether to preserve or demolish that delightfully nostalgic but regrettably dilapidated survival of Victorian ebullience—the West Pier.

The West Pier was among the first of those whimsical but basically practical structures (Sir John Betjeman: 'It provides a walk on the sea without the disadvantage of being sea-sick') which are almost peculiar to England and Wales. As the Mayor of Brighton said at the opening ceremony in October 1866, 'as a means of recreation and health nothing could be more advantageous; and the beautiful pier would remain as an example to future ages of what speculation had done in the nineteenth century.' It is amusing to note that it was attacked by the conservationists of the day because the large toll-houses at its entrance blocked the sea from the view of the residents of Regency Square. Nevertheless as a 'speculation' it was highly successful, the average attendance on a Sunday being 10,000; and piers continued to be so popular as promenades and places of entertainment that another was built at the Steine end of Brighton front in 1899 to replace the Chain Pier that had disappeared three years earlier.

A revival of the West Pier's early glories seemed imminent in 1965 when 97% of the share capital of the West Pier Company was acquired by a large holding company, A.V.P. Industries Ltd., with many property and investment interests including the ownership of two of Brighton's largest hotels, the Metropole and the Bedford. Mr Harold Poster, chairman and managing director of A.V.P., told a local newspaper that he had 'plans for developing Brighton's West Pier as an all-round holiday and conference centre—giving all the enjoyment of being on a luxury cruise', with a heated covered walk to tempt customers into a theatre at the seaward end.

In the event not one of these alterations was made and four years later the company applied for permission to demolish the southern end of the pier.

At a public enquiry in January 1971, structural engineers giving evidence for the pier company and the Corporation stated that the cost of repair would be £650,000; of demolition, £80–100,000.

It was, no doubt, with these figures in mind that Mr Poster indulged in one of those oscillations that were to become characteristic of the West Pier story. He wrote to the local press saying that he had no wish to destroy anything from which residents and others derived pleasure. The pier was not 'commercially viable' but if there was strong feeling that it should be preserved he would donate it to the Regency Society or any other body which could raise the necessary funds for its preservation.

Nothing came of this offer nor of subsequent A.V.P. approaches in which they offered sums of up to £300,000 provided the Corporation entered into an irrevocable undertaking to meet any repair costs in excess of that amount.

Just before Christmas 1974, the Council's Policy and Resources Committee recommended that 'no action be taken' on the West Pier. This—and a gossip paragraph in the London *Times* assuming that the pier's demise was now a foregone conclusion—sparked off a protest movement which began as an ancillary of the Brighton Society but then continued its own vigorous existence under the leadership of Mr John Lloyd, originally a Londoner (like many of Brighton's more spirited devotees).

A petition bearing 4,000 signatures, backed up by some colourful protest marches, persuaded the Council to postpone a decision (which they have been doing ever since), to the relief of the West Pier campaigners and the exasperation of A.V.P. The Council with a list of 1,400 families waiting for houses has a strong lobby against spending money on what non-sympathisers call a 'Victorian frivolity', while a friendlier Councillor epitomised the consensus when he said: 'Everyone wants to save the pier but no one wants to pay for it.'

Money, as in most conservation matters, is the root of the problem. At one stage A.V.P. industries were willing to sell the pier to the Council for a peppercorn price of £1, offering at the same time £50,000 a year for five years towards the cost of repair. The Council believe it would cost £2,000,000 to restore the pier. The campaigners claim an initial expenditure of £600,000 could save it (just over twice the cost of demolition at current prices). The local Chamber of Commerce and Trade considers that 'from a practical and commercial point of view there is no point in keeping it going', whereas the Campaign's sponsors believe that such attractions as a Continental café, a banqueting hall, a cabaret club and a children's theatre could—even with maintenance costs at £42,000 a year for 20 years and £30,000 a year thereafter—produce an annual quarter of a million a year for the Council by 1990 when all loans had been repaid.

In this, as in most other matters affecting the future of the town, it is worth studying what the Tems reports have to say on the subject. In 1973 visitors showed little interest in the piers although the air of decay surrounding the West Pier drew unfavourable comment. But the 1974 report showed an increase in the 'Good' rating which, Mr Tems says, 'is probably due to the nostalgia which is so much expressed these days for piers and other old buildings'. Among the sympathetic comments were: 'Pity they are falling down'; 'Should be preserved'; 'Especially English'; and 'Different'.

All evidence points to the need for Brighton and towns like it to preserve their 'difference', however much they respond to modern requirements. To-day Brighton has half a million staying visitors a year and ten million day trippers; more overseas visitors stay in Brighton than in any other town outside London. But there is no lack of resorts eager to oust Brighton from this favoured position should those in positions of authority be too short-sighted in their strategy.

One of the changes that has occurred in the pattern of visits since the war has been the growth of conference business. The British Association for the Advancement of Science held its annual conference in the Dome as long ago as 1874 (when the audience included the exiled Napoleon III) but until recent times such gatherings were of minor importance in the economy of the town.

This is no longer so. In 1946 12,500 delegates attended 25 conferences; by 1975 the number of conferences and exhibitions had risen to 286 (19 of them international). They had a total of 59,750 delegates, a number which can probably be increased by a half if one includes their entourage, the press and exhibition staff.

For years the main conference venues have been the Dome (the building on the Pavilion estate originally built as palatial accommodation for the Prince Regent's horses) and the Hotel Metropole with its £1½ million Exhibitions Centre (owned by A.V.P.).

Now £9 million has been spent on a new sea-front building, the Brighton Centre, where still more conferences and exhibitions are being held. With simultaneous translation equipment and studio space for radio and television commentators, it is clearly making a bid for the international market. The largest centre of its kind in Britain, its main hall takes 5,000 delegates (or provides 1,951 square metres of exhibition space) and the secondary hall 800 delegates (743 square metres for exhibitions). This puts Brighton well up in the conference league (the Centre Internationale de Paris at Port Maillot has maximum seating of only 4,000). It already has bookings up to 1984, including four annual conferences of the Labour Party and four of the Conservative Party.

It would be unjust to create the impression that all of Brighton Council and their officials are so bemused with new projects that the aesthetic and commercial value of old buildings escapes them. Already the town has eleven 'conservation areas' which include nearly 2,000 'listed buildings' of special architectural and historical interest and in 1976 the Council issued for public discussion a proposal to extend five of the old areas and create five new ones, so that much of Victorian Brighton might be preserved.

But the fact that there is is as yet no sign of a reprieve for the West Pier* is a reminder that only a constant dialogue with the conservation societies is likely to dissuade some of those who govern the town's fortunes from pinning all their faith for the future to bigger, better conference halls and yacht-harbours. These are novelties that other seaside towns not only in Britain but all over Europe are already building or thinking of building. Like international airports they are architectural siblings barely distinguishable one from another, and when every resort is equally well provided with such modern amenities, it will be the attributes recognisably peculiar to a town that will govern its being chosen whether for a holiday, a conference or a place in which to learn a language.

Although Brighton has subsidiary advantages to which I will come in a moment, its claims to 'difference' are that it has sea in front of it, green hills behind it and a pleasant variety of architecture of several periods meeting the eye not only in the admired squares and crescents but in unexpected, unpromising corners.

The *East Sussex County Structure Plan* in which—after a long and patient

---

*The West Pier Company (an A.V.P. subsidiary) went into liquidation in May 1977.

process of 'public participation'—the County Council attempts the thankless task of plotting a way ahead that will do the most good to the greatest number, comes out strongly, as it should, on the side of Downland preservation. From this, as they see it, stems the logic of 'containing' (i.e. limiting) the ability of Brighton and Hove to provide more jobs, because more employees mean more houses and consequent pressures for a further invasion of the countryside.

This limitation is designed to govern offices as much as factories and here it impinges critically on another problem which the County Council's own report throws into sharp focus:

'At the upper end of the housing market there are signs that the erection of substantial numbers of new flats in Brighton and Hove is having the effect of making uneconomic the preservation in use of the fine terraces, squares and crescents which give these places much of their distinctive character. There is little possibility of these properties being properly maintained if they are vacated by reasonably well-to-do occupants and further study is needed to determine the economics of their retention.'

Because it is part of the sea-front shop-window of the two towns the western end of Brunswick Terrace is the area currently attracting most publicity in this context. Behind their crumbling façade these buildings are rotting away (inside one of them there is a clear drop from the fourth floor to the basement). The development company that owns them is going into liquidation; a banking corporation that holds a substantial mortgage on the properties claims that their continued use as flats will not produce an income that would make it worthwhile to restore them to their former Georgian elegance, so they have been seeking planning permission to convert them to offices.

So, 30 years later, Brunswick Terrace is again the main concern of the Regency Society which it brought to birth.

'No solution has yet been found to this problem', said their annual report for 1975, 'but it seems clear that the most practical method of saving the houses would be likely to involve office use of some kind, which is prohibited by the Brunswick Square Act of 1830.' A year later the Society was able to report that a new survey had indicated the possibility of restoration—as flats—for something over a million pounds and that the Historic Buildings Council had made a substantial offer towards the cost of the work. 'Though there is as yet no cut and dried solution in sight . . . '

said the report, 'everyone prefers the idea of dwellings rather than offices in the Terrace'. The debate continues.

In Brighton the debate always continues. Even in 1827 the Comte de La Garde found it to be 'a town above all where everything—whether it be a parish meeting or a debate at Westminster—is analysed, atomised and criticised'. This is even truer to-day when the town has an evening paper, a weekly paper and a local radio station, each of them mindful of its civic responsibilities (and the fact that controversy makes good 'copy'). Because no one lobby ever completely silences all the others the town is preserved from the sterile perfection of those immaculate villages that no longer have any villagers.

Failure invariably attends any attempt to pin its future to a single objective—as a holiday resort, a conference centre, a dormitory town, a nest of pedagogues, a Mecca for upper-income-bracket yachtsmen, a climatically commendable refuge for the aged or a hive of industry (its manufactures range from teleprinters to hand-made replicas of mediaeval musical instruments).

This hybridism would make the first half of Samuel Smiles' prissiest maxim an appropriate sub-title for this book. Brighton *is* a 'place for everything', whatever your temperament or favourite pursuit (or whichever period of English history invites your curiosity), but the tidy-minded will be disappointed if they expect to find 'everything in its place'. Indeed it is Brighton's consistent unpredictability that constitutes its strongest appeal to its admirers. It has its advertised attractions like the annual festival of opera, concerts and drama or the parade of veteran cars each November, but there are many casual pleasures that come as a bonus to these: a famous actress's face catching your eye in the supermarket; village green cricket in the shadow of Stanmer parish church; a handsome wrought-iron balcony in an otherwise sleazy street; hang-glider adepts soaring like Icarus over the Devil's Dyke; cheap tomatoes, second-hand gumboots and tempting antiques at the Saturday morning flea-market in Upper Gardner Street. And it will remain a patchwork of surprises so long as it continues to breed (and import) enthusiasts. No other town provides so perfect a demonstration of Bertrand Russell's theory that 'every isolated passion is, in isolation, insane; sanity may be defined as a synthesis of insanities.'

APPENDIX A

Suggestions for Further Reading

A good starting point for further reading on Brighton is to familiarise one-self with the history of the county as a whole. I would recommend two books, different in style but each excellent in its own way: Marcus Crouch's *Heritage of Sussex* (1969) and J. R. Armstrong's *A History of Sussex* (1974).

For early history the standard and unrivalled work is *The Archaeology of Sussex* (1954) by E. Cecil Curwen,* but a very readable and stimulating book covering the period from the pre-Roman Iron Age to the coming of the Saxons is Barry Cunliffe's *The Regni* (1973). Those interested in visiting archaeological sites should get hold of James Dyer's *Southern England: An Archaeological Guide* (1973).

Still, in my view, an outstanding example of how local history should be written is Charles Thomas-Stanford's *Sussex in the Great Civil War and the Interregnum, 1642—1660,* but this has not been re-printed since its original edition in 1910 and so—unless you live in Sussex—can probably only be obtained for you by a co-operative librarian from some central collection or by an antiquarian bookseller with good contacts.

Dealing with Brighton's history in broader terms (and more easily accessible) are Clifford Musgrave's comprehensive and richly detailed *Life in Brighton* (1970) and the scholarly *Brighton: Old Ocean's Bauble* (1975) in which Edmund M. Gilbert covers the growth and ups-and-downs of the town from the advent of Dr Russell to the 1950's.

Of the books on the Regency two of the most enjoyable are *Brighton* by Osbert Sitwell and Margaret Barton (1935) and *Mrs Fitzherbert* by Anita Leslie (1960); while the same period is covered—with fascinating detail on the development of the Pavilion (and its post-Regency vicissitudes)—

---

*A new publication by the British Council for Archaeology is scheduled for 1978.

in Musgrave's *The Royal Pavilion: A Study in the Romantic* (1951).

The ensuing phase—of great importance architecturally—is covered, with the erudition one would expect of its author, in *Fashionable Brighton: 1820–1860* by Antony Dale (1967).

An engaging record of *Victorian and Edwardian Brighton from Old Photographs* (1972) is made up principally from the private collection of a Brighton resident, Mr J. S. Gray, and has an introduction by Sir John Betjeman (who first stayed at the Old Ship in 1918). A useful companion to this is the B.B.C. publication, *Victorian Sussex* by John Lowerson (1972).

Especially to be commended to those who would like to explore Brighton and its outskirts on foot in search of interesting buildings and their historical associations is Antony Dale's *About Brighton*. Published by the Regency Society (there is a 1976 re-print) at a modest price, it is small enough to fit into a coat-pocket and compendious enough to provide itineraries for several days.

A reader wishing to make his own investigations into Brighton's past (or the past of any other town in the United Kingdom for that matter) will, if this is a new field for him, be well advised to establish the groundwork of the subject by reading G. M. Trevelyan's *English Social History* and then go on to study the useful information on 'sources'—what they are, where to look for them and how to use them—which is to be found in J. J. Bagley's *Historical Interpretation* (1972).

APPENDIX B

Some Places to Visit

ANNE OF CLEVES' HOUSE, LEWES. (Sussex Archaeological Trust).
Timber-framed building containing domestic and folk material including a wide range of Sussex ironwork. Tel: Lewes 4610.

ARUNDEL CASTLE, ARUNDEL.
Castle, including the Keep, Private Chapel, Barons' Hall, Picture Gallery and Armoury. Tel: Arundel 883136 or 882173.

BARBICAN HOUSE MUSEUM, LEWES. (Sussex Archaeological Trust).
Archaeological Museum with prehistoric, Roman and Anglo-Saxon exhibits; Sussex pictures and prints. The house is Elizabethan with later additions. Tel: Lewes 4379.

BATEMAN'S, BURWASH. (National Trust. 13 miles south of Tunbridge Wells, off A.265).
This seventeenth-century Sussex ironmaster's house was Rudyard Kipling's home after he left Rottingdean. Exhibition of manuscripts. His study and rooms are as he left them. Tel: Burwash 882302.

BATTLE ABBEY, BATTLE.
Scene of the Battle of Hastings, where King Harold was defeated by William the Conqueror.

BIGNOR, ROMAN VILLA AND MUSEUM. (6 miles south of Petworth, between A.285 and A.29).
One of the largest Roman villas in Britain. Has some fine mosaics. A museum contains model, plans and relics found at villa. Tel: Sutton 259.

BLUEBELL RAILWAY, SHEFFIELD PARK. (Situated on the A.275 Lewes–East Grinstead road).
Vintage engines and coaches run through five miles of Wealden scenery between Sheffield Park and Horsted Keynes. Museum of historic railway relics. Tel: Newick 2370.

BRIGHTON ART GALLERY & MUSEUM.
Housed in the group of buildings originally designed as stables and 'rid-

ing house' for the Prince Regent. Fine collection of prints and drawings of Brighton from 1750 onwards. Adroit presentation of the town's development as a seaside resort in the attractive 'Brighton Beautiful' exhibition. Tel: Brighton 63005.

CUCKFIELD PARK, CUCKFIELD. (¼ mile south of Cuckfield Village on the A.272).

Elizabethan house and gatehouse built by one of the Sussex iron-masters. Period features include a superbly carved screen, open well staircase, magnificent plaster ceilings and panelling. Tel: Haywards Heath 3198.

DANNY, HURSTPIERPOINT. (midway between Hassocks and Hurstpierpoint, on B.2116).

House completed in 1595. Has fine Great Hall, paintings and ancient books. Tel: Hurstpierpoint 833000.

DEVIL'S DYKE, near POYNINGS.

Famous beauty spot, 711 feet above sea-level, north of Brighton. Site of Iron Age fort.

FIRLE PLACE, FIRLE. (5 miles south-east of Lewes off A.27).

Mainly Georgian, but retaining Tudor 'core'. Famous collection of pictures, porcelain and furniture. Home of Viscount Gage's family for 500 years. Tel: Chiddingly 466 or Glynde 256.

FISHBOURNE ROMAN PALACE AND MUSEUM. (Sussex Archaeological Trust. 1½ miles west of Chichester, off A.27).

The largest Roman residence yet found in Britain and the only one built in true Italian style. Many mosaic-floored rooms. Probably palace of local king, Tiberius Claudius Cogidubnus. Important finds on display. Tel: Chichester 85859.

GLYNDE PLACE, GLYNDE. (4 miles south-east of Lewes, off A.27).

Beautiful example of sixteenth-century architecture in picturesque village of Glynde. Pictures by Hoppner, Lely and Zoffany. Historic documents dating from twelfth century. Tel: Glynde 229 or Lewes 2957.

HASTINGS CASTLE, WEST HILL, HASTINGS.

Norman castle built after the Battle of Hastings on the site of one of William the Conqueror's wooden forts.

LEWES CASTLE, LEWES. (Sussex Archaeological Trust).

Norman castle with a shell keep. Tel: Lewes 4379.

NEWTIMBER PLACE, HASSOCKS. (7 miles north of Brighton, between A.23 and A.281).

Moated seventeenth-century house at the foot of the Downs. Octagonal late seventeenth-century dovecote to hold some hundreds of birds. Tel: Hurstpierpoint 833104.

PARHAM, PULBOROUGH. (2 miles west of Storrington on A.283).

Fine Elizabethan house in Downland setting. Important collection of Elizabethan, Jacobean and Georgian portraits. Fine furniture and needlework. Tel: Storrington 2021.

PARSONAGE ROW COTTAGES, WORTHING. (Sussex Archaeological Trust. In the High Street, West Tarring, Worthing).

Group of three fifteenth-century cottages, containing museum. Tel: Worthing 36385.

PETWORTH HOUSE, PETWORTH. (National Trust. 5½ miles east of Midhurst, at junction of A.272 and A.283).

Built 1686–1696 by the 6th Duke of Somerset. Notable picture collection, furniture and thirteenth-century chapel. Stands in large park. Tel: Petworth 42207.

PEVENSEY CASTLE, PEVENSEY. (3 miles east of Eastbourne).

Mediaeval castle enclosed by Roman walls. It was here that William of Normandy landed in 1066. The Romans had built a fortress on the same spot 800 years earlier.

POLEGATE WINDMILL. (Eastbourne and District Preservation Trust. 4 miles north of Eastbourne, west of A.22).

Tower windmill built in 1817; restored in 1967 with all its machinery intact. Collection of milling 'bygones'. Tel: Eastbourne 54845.

PRESTON MANOR, PRESTON PARK, BRIGHTON.

This old manor house was originally built about 1250 and re-built in 1739. It was presented to Brighton in 1932 by the late Sir Charles and Lady Thomas-Stanford, whose ancestors had lived there for nearly 200 years. The rooms are arranged, as far as possible, as they existed in the lifetime of the donors, with their period furniture, silver, glass, china, etc. Tel: Brighton 552101.

ROYAL PAVILION, BRIGHTON.

Seaside palace of the Prince Regent (later George IV), containing dazzling interiors superbly restored. Decorations in the 'Chinese taste'. Regency furniture and works of art. Many pieces on loan from H.M. the Queen. Tel: Brighton 63005.

ST. MARY'S, BRAMBER. (between Shoreham and Steyning).

Mediaeval building classified by the Ministry of Housing as 'the best example of timber-framing of the late fifteenth century in Sussex'. Rare seventeenth-century painted panelling; painted wall-leather of same period. Period furniture, lace and costumes. Tel: Steyning 813158.

SACKVILLE COLLEGE, EAST GRINSTEAD.

Early Jacobean almshouse with banqueting hall and chapel, built round quadrangular courtyard. Founded by the 2nd Earl of Dorset in 1609. Antique furniture. Tel: East Grinstead 25436.

SHEFFIELD PARK. (4 miles north-east of Uckfield, on A.275).

This estate originally belonged to Earl Godwin, the father of the Saxon King Harold. The present house is basically Tudor, its 'Gothick' appearance being due to alterations in 1775–78. Tel: Danehill 531.

WEALD AND DOWNLAND OPEN AIR MUSEUM, SINGLETON. (Near Chichester, off the A.286 road to Goodwood Racecourse).

Museum of historic buildings from the Weald and Downland area in Kent, Surrey, Sussex and Hampshire. Displays of rural crafts—hurdle-making, charcoal-burning, blacksmithing, etc. Tel: Singleton 348.

WILMINGTON PRIORY. (Sussex Archaeological Trust. 3 miles north-west of Eastbourne, off A.22).

Remains of twelfth-century priory with agricultural museum. Close by is the Long Man of Wilmington, a figure 230 feet high, cut out of the turf on the side of the Downs; date uncertain.

NOTE: The times of opening and the charges for admission have not been given, as these could be subject to change. Up-to-date information on these may be obtained from Brighton's Resort and Conference Department, Marlborough House, Old Steine, Brighton, BN1 1EQ. Tel: Brighton 29801.

Index